Pop Fleyes

Pop Fleyes

Bob Popovics's approach to saltwater fly design

Ed Jaworowski
and
Bob Popovics

Photographed by Ed Jaworowski

STACKPOLE
BOOKS

Published by
STACKPOLE BOOKS
An imprint of The Globe Pequot Publishing Group, Inc.
64 South Main Street
Essex, CT 06426
www.stackpolebooks.com

Distributed by NATIONAL BOOK NETWORK

First paperback edition 2014

Cover photo by Ed Jaworowski
Cover design by Caroline M. Stover
All photos by Ed Jaworowski unless otherwise credited
Illustrations by Dave Hall

Library of Congress Cataloging-in-Publication Data

Jaworowski, Ed
Pop fleyes : Bob Popovics's approach to saltwater fly design / Ed Jaworowski and Bob Popovics ; photographed by Ed Jaworowski.-- 1st ed.
p. cm.
Includes bibliographic references (p.).
ISBN 0-8117-1247-8
1. Flies, Artificial. 2. Fly tying. 3. Saltwater fly fishing. I. Popovics, Bob. II. Title.
SH451 .J28 2001
688.7'9124--dc21

00-061204

ISBN-13: 978-0-8117-1439-6 (pbk)

Printed in India

For my wife, Michele.
Without her love, encouragement, and support,
this project could not have happened.
—Ed

For my wife, Alexis,
who has always allowed me the freedom
to pursue my fly-fishing passion.
—Bob

Contents

Foreword

It has been my very great pleasure to travel much of the fly-fishing world the past forty years. At seminars, clinics, fishing lodges, and other places that we fishermen hang out, I have watched some of the finest fly tiers in the world. I have been tying since 1947, and when I see the talent that some of these people possess, I am truly humbled. But one tier stands out above all others, so far as I am concerned.

What is a truly accomplished fly tier? It is a person who can sit at a vise and turn out remarkable flies, either imitative or attractor, but with fine craftsmanship. Despite their skills, most such tiers are tying patterns developed over the years by others. But a truly great tier is more than this. In my mind, Bob Popovics is one of these.

I believe that Bob is the most innovative fly tier I have ever known. Some of my very good fly-tying friends are renowned throughout the fly-fishing world for their skill at the vise—and I envy their skill. But rarely do they conceive a totally new technique. This is where Bob Popovics excels. He has invented new tying concepts never before considered. His use of materials that were foreign to fly tying, and doing so in novel ways, has resulted in flies that are both fish catchers and innovative. Every time I see Bob and we talk fly tying, Bob shows me a new fly, technique, or idea about tying.

I first met Bob many years ago at a Saltwater Fly Rodders of America conclave when he was a very young man. We worked on his casting, and he has become a great caster. One of his most revered friends, Ed Jaworowski, is also a longtime and great personal friend of mine. Both of these men are among the best of fly casters and fly fishermen. Ed is one of the most talented men I know (anybody that can sing opera, drink beer with the guys on the beach, and teach Latin is a rare person, indeed). Ed is a superb photographer. He and Bob have worked for more than three years in developing this book. Ed wanted the world to know the fantastic work that Bob has done over the years in the field of fly tying.

But this is not just a fly-tying book, of which there are many fine ones. It is much more. I promise that if you thoroughly read this book, even if you never tie a fly, you will improve your fish-catching skills. It's true there is much about tying in this book—supported by hundreds of Ed's excellent photos. The instructions are as good as you can get. Many tying books skimp on some sequences and often skip over or leave out little techniques that are vital to properly dressing the fly. Bob and Ed include every step in pictures and words, and why each step is important.

In addition to tying the flies, there are explanations as to why these flies were developed—so that they will catch fish for the angler. Many fishing techniques related to the patterns are included—which alone are worth the price of the book. Let me just cite one example. The authors point out that different flies require different retrieves. Mullet, squid, and shrimp all act differently in the water, and you need to know how the pattern you tied should be retrieved.

Many professional tiers have copied Bob's work, even to putting their own names on the flies. I believe that is the best compliment he could receive. Once you begin to use and digest this book, you will surely think it is one of the most important in your fishing library.

Lefty Kreh

Preface

This is not a book about how to tie saltwater flies. It deals exclusively with how Bob Popovics ties his own creations, collectively known as Pop Fleyes, and how he thinks about fly designs. Hence, you will find no instructions here for tying a Lefty's Deceiver, Clouser Deep Minnow, or any of the many other important fly designs, which we also use and to which we all owe so much. Nor is this another "recipe" book, showing completed flies and listing materials needed to fashion them. Most especially, *Pop Fleyes* is not a *tour de force,* simply showcasing Bob's considerable fly-tying abilities.

The theme of this book is creativity with purpose. It represents a way of perceiving, based on the premise that form always follows function. The "why" of every technique is paramount. No tying step is employed without some useful purpose, and when Bob says "stack the hair just this way" or "trim it at this point," rest assured he has tried it every other way before deciding his method makes a particular fly float, sink, swim, act, or cast better.

Some thirty years ago, Butch Colvin gave Bob Popovics his first fly-tying lessons in Seaside Park, New Jersey. I had been tying trout and bass flies for fifteen years at the time, but my saltwater fly-fishing experience was slight and my saltwater tying experience virtually nonexistent. During the thirty years we have fished, tied flies, and traveled together, I have come to subscribe wholeheartedly to Bob's way of thinking about fly design. My role has been largely that of a sounding board, offering reactions, criticisms, and suggestions for improvements. While I conventionally use the editorial "we" in describing the tying procedures, nearly all the ideas as described here originated with Bob. My text, written in collaboration with him, attempts to capture and convey those ideas.

We assume that readers of this text will have had some tying experience. We therefore have forgone elementary instructions, such as attaching thread to the hook and whip-finishing the completed fly. On the other hand, to assist tiers in fashioning their own versions of these fly designs, we have made every attempt to illustrate Bob's tying procedures with uncommon detail, trying to capture with still photographs the effectiveness of his *Pop Fleyes* videos. Whenever we felt that drawings could better communicate a point, we employed artist-angler Dave Hall to draw original illustrations. We include historical comments on the evolution of these flies, illustrations and discussion of natural saltwater baits, and random thoughts on tools and materials. Additionally, we've interspersed in the text fishing tips relating to the use of the flies, and photos of fishing them and fish caught on them. With no apologies to those who enjoy tying just for the sake of tying, we believe there is no point to all the effort involved unless directed to the end of fishing them, and we want to reinforce that point constantly.

In the end, this collaboration is, in part, a method of payment for all the help, ideas, and encouragement we have received from so many fly-fishing friends and acquaintances, past and present. In these pages, we hope to share some of our thinking about artificial flies and fly fishing. We hope that those who read and study these pages will adopt and adapt some of these ideas—and pass them on—and in so doing, derive more enjoyment and satisfaction from the sport.

Ed Jaworowski
Chester Springs, Pennsylvania

Acknowledgments

In addition to our wives, Michele and Alexis, to whom this volume is dedicated, we offer our sincerest thanks and appreciation especially to the following:

Lynn Tolleson, for his indispensable photographic advice and assistance.

Lefty Kreh, for additional photographic assistance and more suggestions, encouragement, and ongoing help than we can repay.

Dave Hall, for lending his creative artistry to this project with his line drawings.

Judith Schnell, editorial director of Stackpole Books, who insisted we do this book, and editor Jon Rounds, for his painstaking attention to details.

Al Quattrocchi, graphic designer, for lending his Grammy award-winning skills to this effort.

Andy Renzetti, for the great fly-tying vises and tools that make our sport so much better.

Nick Curcione and Bob Clouser, two great anglers, for their suggestions and help with testing fly designs.

Lance Erwin, who has probably caught more fish on Pop Fleyes than any of us.

Joe Cavanaugh, for years of positive support and enthusiasm.

Butch Colvin, for a birthday gift of vise, tools, and materials, and for early fly-tying lessons.

"Uncle" Fred Schrier, who instilled a love of the sport.

Poul Jorgensen, for early tying instruction and encouragement.

The Atlantic Saltwater Flyrodders of Seaside Park, New Jersey, of which we are both charter members, and the memory of the Saltwater Fly Rodders of America, Chapter One, headquartered in Seaside Park during the 1960s and 1970s. Our friends in both of these organizations have enriched our fishing and our lives immeasurably.

DIGITAL IMAGING BY AL QUATTROCCHI, TORNADO DESIGN

An Atlantic silverside (top), a Surf Candy (middle), and the two images superimposed (bottom) to show how closely the Pop Fleye imitates the natural.

Chapter One

Designing Pop Fleyes

A BIT OF HISTORY

The flies illustrated and discussed in these pages represent ways of thinking about artificials as much as they do ways of tying them. Bob claims, "I never was successful with fly patterns when I tried to come up with something 'clever.' Any successes I had only came when there was a need to be answered or a problem to be solved." The following two episodes, a bit of history, if you will, highlight the Pop Fleyes approach. More than simply slices of nostalgia, they illustrate our first rules of fly design.

About 1970, a year after being introduced to saltwater fly fishing by Fred Schrier, Butch Colvin, and some other members of Chapter One of the Saltwater Flyrodders of America, headquartered in Seaside Park, New Jersey, Bob started tying flies. A birthday gift of a vise and other basics was complemented with a few elementary lessons. Ken Bay's *Tying Salt Water Flies* was his Bible and in many ways has been an inspiration for this book. As if a portent of the future, Mark Sosin's Blockbuster fly, which used epoxy to protect its many thread wraps, and then Hal Janssen's Hamada Silverside, an epoxy-covered balsa minnow, caught his attention. He "played" with epoxy, as he puts it, hoping to produce some sort of indestructible fly. Bluefish had always taken a great toll on flies, and quality fishing time was missed changing flies, since blitzing fish can come and go in a hurry. His earliest flies caught fish, but in retrospect, they were quite crude. He hadn't even put eyes on them, since realism was not a concern at the time. They were purely utilitarian flies. Yet even then, Bob sensed that epoxy had more potential than simply making durable fly bodies, but he hadn't yet learned to manage the drips, sags, and tackiness of the messy stuff to his satisfaction. He did note, however, the translucent effects gained from covering tinsel or hair with epoxy, but it would be a while before he would fully appreciate and explore the characteristics of the material that would lend realism, translucence, and form to his creations. He put his epoxy flies on the back burner and, for a while, focused his efforts in another direction.

Sitting in between fly-tying great Poul Jorgensen and fly-fishing legend Charles Waterman at a fly show in the early seventies, tyro tier Bob Popovics successfully addressed his first major tying problem. His work eventually caught the attention of celebrities, and this experience established a precedent that would eventually define the essence of his approach to tying.

Striped bass feast on large herring and menhaden (commonly known as mossbunker or simply bunker), and surf casters who were converting to the fly rod wanted flies to take the place of the large Atom, Creek Chub, and Gibbs plugs they cast. Design was all important, the problems many. Suitable materials for really large flies were not readily available, and no one Bob knew had ever seriously explored the area. The Joe Brooks Blonde series, the Harold Gibbs Striper Fly, and the Lefty's Deceiver, a rather recent creation at the time, summarized the arsenal of most eastern anglers. They were all good flies, but bucktail and feathers couldn't supply the proportions Bob required. Size, weight, form, action, and castability all had to be considered. Beginning from his long familiarity with and remarkable sense of baitfish proportion and shape, he first conceived what he required, then set about to solve the problems.

For generations, fly size had always been determined by hook size. A size 12 Royal Wulff was understood to be tied on a size 12 dry-fly hook; a larger fly required a larger hook. A size 2/0 or 3/0, the largest practical hook most people could then comfortably cast, limited fly size to perhaps 6 inches. Bob decided to think like a bait fisherman. Instead of attaching all materials directly to the hook, the traditional approach, his concept was for a fly largely tied apart and then attached to the hook, not unlike the idea of inserting a hook into the front end of a large natural bait. He placed two fly-tying vises about 18 inches apart and stretched a heavy piece of monofilament between them. He held a tuft of short bucktail along one side of the mono with his left hand, and by repeatedly bringing the bobbin and thread up the near side of the mono, dropping it behind the mono, and then

An early Big Bunker Fly, over 11 inches long, tied thirty years ago. It required extensive tying procedures but broke with traditional thinking.

Early epoxies, now brown with age, featured painted eyes and painted feathers representing gill covers.

pulling it tight, he secured the bucktail to the mono. He continued attaching successive tufts of light blue and purple hair along the mono for a distance of 8 or 9 inches. He repeated the process on a second piece of mono, using white bucktail. Then he attached two dark hackle points to the end of a third strand and slipped braided silver piping material over the mono, leaving the tail protruding. The three mono strands were tied together at both ends and the front ends attached near the bend of a large hook. The top strand, with the colored bucktail, formed the back of the bogus bait, while the white hairs formed the belly. The silver middle line added flash and gave some rigidity to the fly. To complete the body, he wrapped heavy chenille around the hook shank, added large glass doll eyes, then additional bucktail and some herl to maintain the front taper. He even coated the final wraps with epoxy, which in retrospect also seems portentous.

Some laughed at the fly, but those who didn't asked, "Why didn't I think of that?" The original Big Bunker Fly was not tier friendly, for it involved a lot of tying, much more so than the Blockbuster or Hi-Tie, and a lot of material. The chenille retained a lot of water, and the glass eyes were heavy. Also, if a thread was broken, the fly would start to unravel. But techniques in the design were groundbreaking. Huge size, by early standards, was achieved without the materials available today. More importantly, it represented a departure from traditional thinking. No longer limited by material length and hook size, here was a bona fide striped bass fly nearly a foot long, with a three- to four-inch-wide profile. This creation, albeit unwieldy, pointed in a new direction. The fly could still be cast comfortably about 50 feet on a number 11 rod, and Bob laughingly confesses to only one flaw in his plan: "I couldn't convince any of my surf fishing buddies to tease a 40-pound striper to the surface with a live bunker or herring and then pull it away from the fish at the last instant so that I could cast a fly to it."

Jump to the mid 1980s. Bob again began experimenting with the idea of making more durable fly bodies. He determined this time to master epoxy, to learn how to control it for predictable results. Bob resurrected the old epoxy flies and set about to produce more realistic baitfish imitations virtually impervious to teeth and possessing translucence, but he first had to master the techniques of working with epoxy. This time his experiments produced his first viable minnow imitations. Various tiers were experimenting with epoxy back then, but none of the efforts had gained wide acceptance from fishermen. Epoxy was still used either simply to protect thread wraps or to cast rigid bodies of crabs or other baits. The first practical epoxy Pop Fleyes were born

In the early days, we experimented with all sorts of epoxy flies.

when Bob incorporated the hard material to shape a realistic, translucent minnow body and wedded it with hair, which gave movement. The key lay first and foremost in manipulating and constantly sculpting the body with a bodkin until the material gelled and set.

Eventually, at the Fly Tackle Dealer Show held in Boston in 1989, we showed an assortment of early creations to magazine editor Dick Stewart, himself a great tier. His reaction was terse and enthusiastic: "Write them up for me." The spring 1990 issue of *American Angler and FlyTyer* revealed the first photos and tying instructions and featured them on the cover. We called them Pop Fleyes, concocting a combination of the beginning of Bob's surname and a stylized spelling of flies, based on the dominant eyes. Shortly afterward, as other patterns were born, we adopted the name for the whole series of creations, and the original epoxies we henceforth dubbed Surf Candies. The name was based on the fact that most of our saltwater fishing took place in the local

The newer-generation Shady Lady Squid (center) and Cotton Candy (right) represent far more effective techniques for producing large flies than the original Big Bunker Fly.

New Jersey surf, and the colorful plastic flies reminded us of the hard candies Bob always had at hand near his tying table.

The earliest Surf Candies employed bucktail, and many sported painted eyes and painted feather gill plates and often featured a mylar piping extension with a feather tail, which we later incorporated into the full dress Surf Candy but eliminated in the basic version. Some sand eel imitations even had lead wire wrapped around the shank, which at that time we thought was necessary to make them ride with the hook up, and long extensions made by attaching saddle hackles to monofilament. This was how we achieved greater length before the advent of the many excellent long synthetics we now use. We eventually substituted polar bear hair for the bucktail, then Thompson's UltraHair and Bestway's Super Hair. These afforded greater durability and came in a variety of translucent colors. We also came to learn in time that weighting the shank is not the key to making a fly ride hook up (see the section on Jiggies, page 47).

Reaction to and acceptance of the new flies were instant and overwhelming. We recall the day that Lance Erwin, a crack angler, burst into the tying room with an orange Surf Candy on which he had just landed twenty-five bluefish in the surf. The body was badly scratched and the hair somewhat thinned out, but the fly was otherwise intact. An overcoat of Hard as Nails polish virtually removed all the battle scars, and the fly, looking nearly new, was ready for further usage. Never had we used flies capable of withstanding that degree of torture. Today such flies are routinely accepted. Then it was a staggering accomplishment: one fly outlasting perhaps a dozen conventional streamers or bucktails.

These two examples represent the approach adopted in all subsequent Pop Fleyes creations, which have today developed into a series of tier-friendly flies, covering the needs of inshore and offshore anglers, with applications in fresh water as well. The first and most important lesson to be learned from these experiences is that previsualization of the results you want, based on a predetermined need, is the key to designing and tying worthwhile flies. Second, if you believe the concept is sound, stick with it. Constantly refine your techniques and opportunities, for other ideas and designs will evolve. Trial and error are important. The thinking and techniques applicable to one fly may well be translated and incorporated into

More recent Surf Candies (at top) are lighter, easier, and quicker to tie than early versions with heavy eyes and excess epoxy.

another. All the flies discussed in this book represent continual and ongoing experimentation and refinement. The Surf Candies we tie today are direct descendants of those persistent attempts a generation ago, when epoxy and silicone, now available in most fly shops largely because of Pop Fleyes, could only be purchased in hardware stores. Likewise, the tedious and labor-intensive techniques of the Big Bunker Fly have given way to simpler and more friendly techniques used in the Cotton Candy and other large Pop Fleyes.

Even though the world of fly fishing is vastly different today, and what was then innovative is now accepted as routine, the same principles still hold true: Define problems, don't ever be satisfied with what you've done, try constantly to improve on it.

Successful fly designs are driven by need. Not that it isn't fun to just make something on a whim—but don't expect it to be a classic.

Matching the hatch, saltwater style.

OBSERVATIONS ON IMITATION

Tradition, like cholesterol, comes in good and bad forms—that which enriches and that which inhibits. Unfortunately, bad traditions die hard. Trout fly tiers who were once wedded to unreasonable tradition frowned on dyed materials, insisting that only natural hairs and feathers should be used. No synthetics were allowed, and even dyed materials were considered a desecration. Also, they tolerated no variation from rigidly prescribed patterns. Hence the Quill Gordon, Hendrickson, and Red Quill dry flies, though their individual names persisted, all were tied on the same hook and used precisely the same hackle, wing, and tail. They employed the same tying techniques, shape, and design. Even the slightly varying body materials were used more for color difference than anything else. And fly tying stagnated.

Names of artificials proliferated, even though they represented no substantial difference in design. Anglers insisted upon precise colors, even though all animals in nature vary somewhat. Not all pheasants, horses, or collies are exactly the same color as every other specimen of their species. It strikes us as ludicrous to insist on tying flies based on neat and precise color charts. Eventually, however, many trout anglers did come to appreciate the wisdom of imitating different stages of insects, emergers, cripples, stillborns, and such. Hairwings, no hackles, parachutes, Compara-duns, and other designs employed lessons learned from observation of naturals and were suited to the various waters and conditions under which they would be fished. Tiers had come to accept new techniques and designs, and not until that happened was the sport able to progress.

The saltwater angling scene has been struggling to emerge from its own Dark Ages of late, comparable to that of trouting described above, but a bit more complex. On the one hand, some say that if plain white bucktail tied on a hook will catch a fish, why bother with anything else? Those of a far different mindset maintain that innovation should be given free rein and anything goes.

Change, too, may be good or bad, and so it should not be avoided but controlled. It's beneficial if it is reasonable, starting from a logical plan and aimed at a practical end. Change for no real purpose will lack permanency. The plain white bucktail approach may be fine, until our fishing requires—or the fish request—something more durable, or nonfouling, or larger, or with a different silhouette. Then we must seek a solution based on the specific requirement. In this section, we relate our basic approach to fly tying.

Here's an anecdote to illustrate the point. One evening at a fly-tying club, we were approached by a trout angler who insisted that he had a really great idea for an article for us to write. "Tell us about it." "Well, I have this great nymph that I tie . . ." "What's so great about it?" "It really catches fish." "Well, then, we probably don't need it." His jaw dropped and he stared bewilderingly. We continued, "First, all flies (within reason, of course) catch fish. If you had said that your fly sinks, floats, or casts better, acts differently, absorbs water, sheds water, anything, that's something else."

Thousands of flies are created annually, and it's only natural that their creators fall in love with them. But the fact remains that flies like the Lefty's Deceiver, the Clouser Deep Minnow, the Muddler Minnow, the Dahlberg Diver, the Wulff drys, and some others are classics because they broke new ground. They redirected the course of fly tying and, as a result, fly fishing. They have a common element. They evolved from a need—a need to do something better, something different. Note, we did not say they simply *did* something differently, rather, they answered a need. New fly designs should always strive either to do something previously not possible at all or to do something better than was previously possible, be it ever so small a difference.

You will note, for example, that there are no crab patterns in this book. Not that we haven't come up with our own successful crab patterns. The same goes for our spoon eel. We simply don't think ours are any better than some already out there. For now, at least, we have determined that Del Brown's Permit Crab and Jon Cave's Wobbler fly work satisfactorily and are excellent designs. If, on the other hand, we determine something needs to be refined or reworked, we'll pursue that avenue.

All Pop Fleye designs start with observation. In attempting to mimic nature, we follow the dictate that form must follow function. We cannot imagine a *raison d'être* for making artificial flies except in relation to the world of predator and prey—that is, to the end of fishing them. Otherwise, why would we even tie a fly on a fish

We resort to netting mullet to study them more closely.

hook at all? What would determine our choice of size, shape, color? Pop Fleyes are fishing flies, and they represent problem solving. It doesn't matter so much whether the imitation is realistic or surrealistic, so long as it is based on some attempt to capture the look, size, action, color, or some other characteristic of the natural.

We don't subscribe to rigid patterns. There are too many variables for that. Water clarity, light intensity, depth, currents, turbulence, structure, fish preference, and other factors must be taken into account. Successful designs must allow for ready adjustment to these variables. Fly action, color, buoyancy, sink rate, and silhouette must adapt to ever-changing fishing conditions. Be especially cautious of assuming you have solved a problem after one or two successful outings. Only long-term success, under a wide range of circumstances, counts if you want to create lasting fly designs. Again, consider Lefty's Deceiver and Clouser's Deep Minnow. Don't be overly enthusiastic about a pattern you concoct based solely on its appearance. Can you sense in it something different in terms of function? Flies that don't answer this question rarely catch on. I recall with a smile the day when fishing pal Bill Dickson, an outstanding tier, examined one of the early Pop Fleyes. He studied it

Note the square belly sac, silver stripe, eye, and translucence of this silverside.

This 6-inch Lefty's Deceiver is dwarfed by even one-half of a herring.

carefully and proclaimed with an air of confidence, "I can tie that fly, probably as well." Then his shoulders dropped, and he sighed, "But I can't think of that fly."

Begin by studying the naturals, much the way trout anglers have long studied mayflies and caddisflies. For many years, we have collected, studied, photographed, and filmed bait and fish in their environments. Bob's remarkable videos have produced a library of fish and bait behavior, including revealing underwater scenarios. Fish forms and movements seen this way have changed our perception about baits and how we should imitate them. Some of the features we consider translatable to flies include form, silhouette, translucence, flash, action, color. Part of the challenge, as well as the frustration, lies in the fact that we can never know just which is the most important under a given set of conditions. Therein lies the endless fascination with the sport of fly fishing.

Here is a sample of some specific observations. Note the belly sac on a silverside. It is fully one-half the body length and abruptly truncated at that point. Note the belly portion on some of the epoxy Surf Candies in the next chapter, which replicate this feature. Notice how far forward the eye is, too. Size is another case in point. A 6-inch Lefty's Deceiver seen in the accompanying photo is dwarfed by one-half a herring that has been chopped by a large bluefish. The search for techniques that would enable us to reproduce large bait types led to the development of the Cotton Candy, a large, lightweight, and castable replica.

The dominant eye of many baits warrants attention, and the Pop Fleye Siliclone evolved from a search for matching the rounded head of mullet, while the differences in the walking and swimming legs of shrimp are accounted for by the mixture of UltraHair and hackle found in the Ultra Shrimp. Note the rounded nose of

Excellent design makes this 14-inch Cotton Candy surprisingly easier to cast than expected.

the bay anchovy, the eye position, the silver stripe, and the translucence, all effectively captured by an epoxy Surf Candy. Yet notice that mullet are totally opaque, like the Siliclone.

The dominant eye of natural baits is worth copying.

A bay anchovy, or rainfish, is translucent and sports a silver stripe.

A Siliclone copies the rounded form of the mullet.

Mullet are opaque and of generally uniform color.

Shrimp have different types of legs, which the Ultra Shrimp copies.

We filleted these dead baitfish (a bay anchovy and a round herring) to identify them and better understand translucence.

Note the pearlescence of this menhaden, or bunker.

In our attempt to understand translucence better, we filleted two baits, a bay anchovy and a round herring that had washed onto the beach. It also helped us in identifying the fish. Years ago, the round herring was widely known as "anchovy," which simply isn't true. We now know a lot more about this baitfish. Pearlescence or iridescence is often an important feature we do well to imitate. Some baits have it, especially under certain light conditions. Others lack it.

If all this seems to you like going too far, well maybe sometimes it is. We are convinced that often it is not. At any rate, in the long run, sharpening one's powers of observation and paying attention to detail stimulate creativity and generate further fly development. It is a logical and rational approach to the sport. It's what makes fly fishing more creative than spin fishing.

Decide what quality is most important for your imitation, then adapt techniques and materials to your purpose. If fly design is not consistently successful, note when it is, and modify some feature for other occasions when action, or color, or shape adjustment makes a more successful imitation. This is how you will evolve worthwhile designs. Whether you want to imitate a mullet, sand eel, or herring, start with one of the Pop Fleye designs that follow, and fit it to your experience or perception. Material choices should be dictated by individual fly requirements. Instead of tying flies just because a certain material happens to appeal to our sense of aesthetics, we search for materials to meet the needs of a particular design.

Here are a few more random thoughts that you should consider when fashioning your own flies. Judge your fly by the way it appears in your vise. Many tiers believe that by thoroughly wetting a fly, they can envision what it will look like in water. This simply isn't so. When pulled out of the water, the materials cling together, but when immersed again, they open and resume their original form. Nor does retrieving through the water streamline flies as much as is generally assumed. The Spread Fly, Bucktail Deceiver, and Cotton Candy are all designed on the assumption that they will retain their profiles when fished.

Integrate the components of your flies. Study any natural baitfish, and you will see that "flow" is an important characteristic. Lines of the fly should harmoniously

Wetting a fly can mislead about its appearance. When immersed in water, this fly will assume the shape it had in the vise.

Sometimes durability is important. One bluefish can destroy a well-tied traditional streamer.

Saltwater fish are aggressive; flies have to be tough.

move from one part to the other. We see many copies of the epoxy Surf Candy where the hard body ends abruptly and the hair seems to explode out of it to the rear. Or the hair is cut square like a paintbrush. The lines are not smooth and natural. Recently a tier submitted a 3D fly to us for critiquing. He hadn't seen what stood out to us instantly. We traced the silhouette on a piece of paper and showed it to him. The tier was unaware that the fly lacked harmony of its parts.

The Jiggy (see page 47) is another case in point. There is more to this seemingly simple design than meets the eye. The key to making the parts flow together is the clear mono thread. By using it to secure the eyes, we are able to get by with a single, light coat of epoxy over the wraps. Simply pasted on, even if first creased, the eyes won't adhere to the narrow tied-down neck of the fly; they tend to straighten and stand out like hubcaps. Had we used two coats of epoxy, with the eyes applied after the first coat, the fly would have been too thick there and the flow interrupted. Attention to such details is one of the keys to successful fly design and the very essence of the Pop Fleyes approach.

Some flies require more durability than others. Decide on your needs and then pick your material, whether epoxy, silicone, Soft Body, or simply more durable hair. Anticipate the demands that casting and fishing will make on your flies.

When employing flash in your flies, be aware that many forms of tinsel cling and tangle when wet. The Inner Flash fly (page 101) addresses this problem. And don't overwhelm your flies with flash. For some imitations, just creating highlights or a soft glow is more effective, since fish give off different degrees of reflection under different light conditions. Often, we incorporate little or no flash material into a Siliclone or Semper Fleye we will fish at night. From our underwater observations, we note too that on sunny days, especially in shallow water, baits are very light on top and dark on the bottom, but on overcast days, they are more subdued, with less contrast. Just a touch of flash may draw attention then from predatory fish.

Buoyancy of materials and weight balance also should be understood when designing flies. Weights like lead eyes and cone heads will help sink the fly and give it great jigging action on the retrieve but do not determine whether it rides hook up or hook down, unless, of course, the hair is so sparse as to be negligible. What we are saying is that the wing material, not the weight, is the principal instrument in turning the fly and maintaining its "upside-down" attitude. Understanding this is a key to fashioning successful Jiggies or any other flies that ride hook up. Think of the wing as a mechanical steering and balancing device. The first bonefish either of us ever caught was on a Horror fly, which rode hook up before bead chains were in vogue and lead eyes were invented. A single tuft of bucktail easily turned over a heavy stainless steel hook.

To confirm our idea, we tied a series of flies, using both lead eyes and cones (it made no difference in the results), and tying some without any weight at all, bendback and straight shank. We placed bucktail or fiber wings on the inside of the shank or on the outside. We did the same with lead eyes, until we had every conceivable combination. Without exception, the buoyancy and resistance of the hair determined how the fly rode in the water, not the weight of the eyes or cone. If the hair was placed on the outside of the shank, regardless of any additional weight, the fly rode in "normal fashion" with the bend of the hook down. If the hair was on the inside, it rode hook up.

These are only some of the important considerations of which tiers should be aware. Others will be included throughout the text as we discuss specific designs. Putting all the foregoing together, we have arrived at some guidelines for good fly design. They are condensed and not necessarily in order of priority, for that will change; remember, the variable factors discount firm rules about what features are most important at any one time. These do represent, however, the most important items we take into account when designing flies.

Guidelines for Pop Fleyes Design

- Ease of construction
- Durability
- Castability
- Resistance to fouling
- Profile/shape
- Incorporation of prominent, identifiable features of the natural, including action
- Consideration of where in the water column the fly will be used

Flies that don't make the grade usually fail on one of these counts. A large fly may mimic the size of the natural but, because of poor design, be virtually uncastable. Or a realistic streamer may look great but foul on every third cast.

At the beginning of the tying instructions for each of the major patterns, which begin in chapter 3, we have included a complete materials list but have not specified colors. That is one of the options of the tier in nearly all cases and may be changed according to one of the variables discussed above, such as clarity, water depth, light intensity, or fish preference. We rarely consider specific color an essential of fly design.

As tying is a two-handed operation, in our instructions we distinguish the "tying hand," the tier's dominant hand, from the "materials hand," which normally holds materials in place or manipulates them. We have found this helps tiers in following directions, rather than referring to right or left hand.

We conclude this chapter with a brief survey of some common baitfish, mostly of the east coast, with discussion of their appearances and behaviors. Most have similar counterparts on other coasts. We include this more to help sharpen powers of observation than to serve as a guide to identification or reference work. Tiers should be as familiar as possible with what it is they are imitating.

SALTWATER BAITFISH

Some knowledge of saltwater baitfish will help you understand the direction in which we are going with *Pop Fleyes.* We show here some of the more common baitfish that suggest the range of shapes, forms, and features we attempt to imitate. Fly tiers should always familiarize themselves with how naturals, whether mayflies or menhaden, look and act. After all, regardless of how realistic, impressionistic, or vaguely suggestive our representations might be, a fundamental part of the definition of our sport involves tying artificial counterparts of natural forage on which fish feed. Your tying and fishing will proceed more logically and sensibly if you know something

This Siliclone copies the bulk and color of the mullet.

A sand eel wiggling out of the sand.

Surf Candies tied to imitate sand eels.

A natural and its imitation.

Ed Jaworowski caught this big bass on a large sand eel imitation at Cape Cod.

about those naturals. Logic dictates that you don't throw tiny rainfish imitations or crab imitations to fish chasing chunky mullet or herring.

Generic bucktails and streamers will always catch their share of fish, but imitations that consciously strive to represent *some* feature of the naturals—shape, action, color, size, sparkle—usually score more consistently. A modified version of "matching the hatch," to borrow the popular freshwater phrase, certainly makes the sport more interesting.

The sand eel, properly called the American sand lance and not really an eel at all, has a very elongated body, green or olive to brownish on the back, with shiny silver sides and a white belly. They are plentiful throughout the mid-Atlantic–New England range. Their shape and wiggling, eel-like movements give them their common name. Sand eels burrow into the sand along shallow beaches and sandbars, but a sudden stamp from your foot will send them scurrying out of their hiding places. When washed onto the shore by waves, they quickly try to wriggle back into the sand for protection. They are a

A silverside, or spearing.

prime striper and bluefish food, and many popular patterns are tied to imitate them. We have seen huge stripers chasing specimens of more than 8 inches in New Jersey and Cape Cod waters, but generally we seek to imitate the far more common fish of about 3 or 4 inches.

The Atlantic silverside, or spearing, has as typical a minnow form as there is. A bright silver stripe down the midline of the body typifies the silverside and should be given attention by tiers; incorporating strips of mylar is often a good idea. Their backs are green to bluish olive. The most common size is 2 to 5 inches.

Bay anchovies are similar to spearing but have more white on the head and belly sac, and a slightly more rounded snout. They are popularly known as rainfish because schools often dimple the surface in such a way as to resemble rain lightly falling on the water. Some whimsical fishermen dub schools of the tiniest specimens, which make only the slightest surface disturbances, drizzle fish. Typical size is 2 to 4 inches. Quite translucent, almost transparent in the rear part of their bodies, they too, sport a midline stripe that can look like aluminum foil.

Fly tiers will also do well to focus on their silver-white bellies and dominant eyes when fashioning imitations. In dense schools, the bay anchovies appear brownish or reddish brown. Individual specimens usually exhibit a brownish tan or pinkish tinge on the back. Schooled anchovies tend to hug the shore, and unlike species that scatter when threatened, they pack more closely. Nor do they move on as quickly as some fish, so their arrival can signify good fishing for several days, unless weather pushes them out—or bluefish decimate

Bay anchovies.

Bluefish are shown here blitzing on bay anchovies.

Bay anchovies will draw game fish into easy casting range, often right to the beach.

Baits washed ashore give anglers a chance to study and imitate them.

Note the dominant eyes of these round herring.

them. The Surf Candy, along with its variations, like the Stick Candy, and the Jiggy flies generally imitate sand eels, silversides, and bay anchovies.

With regard to baitfish sizes, incidentally, here's an important observation. What the observer mainly sees, when schools of spearings or anchovies spray into the air, is the dominant white or silver belly sac, which is probably the source of the name white bait, used in some quarters to refer to silversides, anchovies, and similar little baits. Since the rest of their body is quite translucent, the fish generally appear smaller than they actually are, and this should be taken into account when tying or choosing artificials.

Though not so familiar to anglers as many of the other baits, the round herring (the only member of the family with a round cross section) has long been a popular mid-Atlantic forage during the summer and fall. They are common in New Jersey, and Capt. Brian

Horsley informs us that he has come across them along the North Carolina coast as well. The round herring is uniformly silver, with a slightly darker back and obvious overall scaling, and features a dominant eye. Like all the herrings, their flesh is dark, and they lack the translucence of spearing and bay anchovies.

Killifish and mummichogs resemble freshwater chubs in body structure. These killies and mummies are probably the most commonly sold minnows for live baitfishing for fluke and other fish along the mid-Atlantic coast. Their chunky, little bodies display somber, mottled, and striped patterns of green, brown, and olive. In large schools, they inhabit marshes, estuaries, bays, and lagoons, where flounders, weakfish, and young stripers feed on them. We haven't had call to design specific imitations for these fish, but a small Spread Fly (see page 57) in the appropriate colors or a modified version of the baby bunker Inner Flash fly (page 101) work well. Incorporate green and brown into your artificials.

Smelts, capelins, and mackerel represent slightly fuller body types. The first two are not far different from the silversides or anchovies, and modified imitations work well. The Atlantic mackerel (Boston mackerel to some, tinkers when small), however, merits special attention. It has long been a popular live-lining bait with New England striped bass fishermen, and some surf men claim that this oily fish, fresh or salted, is the finest bluefish bait of all. Not strangely, then, fly anglers have actively sought imitations for this popular forage, whose larger size adds to their popularity with tiers. Mackerel are fusiform in shape, cylindrical in cross section, and attractive in color, with blue and green backs laced with wavy black markings, and silver-white bellies.

Even fuller-bodied types, as well as those with wider, flatter profiles, include mullet, sardines, herring, menhaden, and butterfish. While not nearly so common in New England waters, white mullet (finger mullet) and the generally larger striped mullet (corn cobs) rate high in importance from the mid-Atlantic zone southward. Generally round in cross section, they show a somewhat flattened head. By early September, mullet start their southward journey and are one of the most important striped bass and bluefish forage fish for the early half of the fall. They frequently swim in the skinny water tight to the beach, invariably north to south. Corners where jetties meet the beach are thus natural ambush points for hungry game fish. Dorsal colors run from bluish green through olive-brown. There is typically a blue spot near the base of the pectoral fin. The sides and belly are whitish or dull silver. In the water, pods of mullet make a telltale surface wake, and catching them in cast nets is a popular activity along the New Jersey coast in fall. The

The white mullet, commonly called a finger mullet.

Popovics Siliclone was originally tied specifically to imitate this fish.

Herring and menhaden are related and quite similar in appearance. Depending on locale, menhaden are variously called bunker, mossbunker, or pogie (not porgy, which is a different fish). The fish are prolific and travel in very dense schools, which appear nearly black in the water. Summer vacationers bait their crab traps with the oily fish, and most live-lining for striped bass along the coast is done with herring or bunker up to a foot in length, hence large imitations are sometimes in order. Flies incorporating iridescent materials, to mimic the pearlescence of the naturals, are the most realistic. Bunker and herring school to size from little "peanut bunker" to huge mouthfuls a foot long or more, so prepare imitations accordingly. Stripers will invariably select any wounded member from among thousands; work your fly accordingly, with an erratic retrieve. Both are oily fish, bunker more so, and a telltale slick on the surface often marks the location of fish feeding on bunker. This is especially true with regard to bluefish, which chop larger baits in half, letting oils escape, before consuming them.

Sardines, particularly the Spanish sardine, can be important at times. Most herring imitations, if made a bit more slender, will make good sardine imitations. The balao, or ballyhoo, and other halfbeaks, their elongated lower jaw notwithstanding, belong in this group. They are popular forage for dorado and other pelagic species.

Butterfish are quite round in profile and flattened or compressed in cross section, with silvery white sides, blue backs, and smooth skin. A chunk of butterfish has long been a favorite with bait anglers fishing for bluefish because of its ability to stay on a hook and its sweet, delicate flavor. Eastern fish markets dress and sell larger butterfish (larger than the typical 3- to 6-inch size) as table

Menhaden, or mossbunker.

This oily slick marks a school of bluefish feeding on bunker.

Except for the long beak, several common baitfish resemble the size and shape of this balao, or ballyhoo.

Butterfish imitations should have a wide silhouette.

fare, and sea lion trainers often reward their charges with the saucer-shaped fish. Despite these testimonies to their large numbers and wide consumption by game fish, butterfish imitations are few. The butterfish's shape was one of the inspirations for the Spread Fly (see page 57).

Many baitfish appear different from one another in the water. Often you can recognize the type from the color or some habit of the school.

We and others have hauled cast nets onto shore with some surprising results. We have had juvenile jacks, pompano, trigger fish, spotted ribbon fish, needlefish, even bonefish mixed with the usual east coast species. Though these oddities are not common or generally in large numbers, these experiences have made us aware of the diverse bait forms available to the game fish in our waters and affect the way we approach our roles as tiers and fishermen. We have especially noted that during full-scale blitzes, huge onslaughts of predator fish wildly feeding on even larger schools of smaller prey, many additional species get drawn into the melee, creating an uncommon smorgasbord for the predators. Why this is we don't fully understand, but the combined energy of all the fish involved seems to intensify the activity. We also note that contrary to the normal behavior of baits schooling to size when driven by blitzing predators, different sizes of baitfish of the same species are sometimes mixed together. We have had bay anchovies an inch and a half, more than 2 inches, and nearly 4 inches all mixed in the same bunch. At any rate, for us, the lessons are obvious: Game species are feasting on more forage types than we generally imagine.

Of course, there are many other baits, but some are obvious to most anglers and quickly identified, like shrimp, squid, crab, or eels. Yet others are similar enough to one of the baits described above that the same imitations or slight variations will work just fine. For example,

Mullet swimming through a wave.

Atlantic silversides, or spearing.

Bay anchovies appear brownish in schools.

Bunker pack densely and appear nearly black in schools.

This small Florida pompano is representative of the many unusual fish that turn up in the midst of east coast blitzes. They are seemingly attracted into the schools of other baits and become forage for the predator fish.

This squid was caught on a squid jig. Squid attach themselves to the bright lure and are hauled from the water before they can unwrap their tentacles, giving us a good chance to study them.

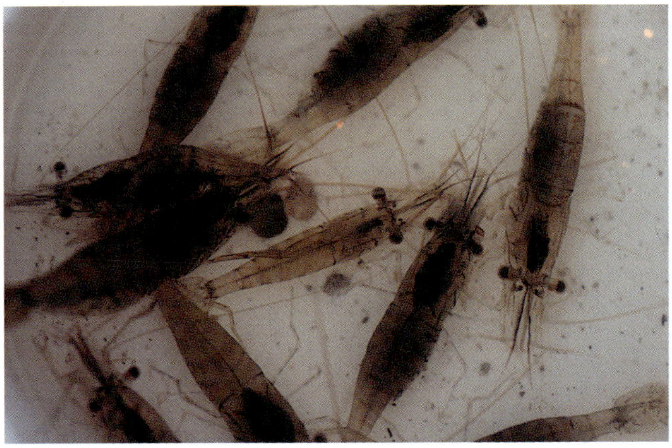

Grass shrimp, so effectively imitated by the Ultra Shrimp, are a mainstay of inshore game fish.

Most crab species share a common shape, varying only in color. Many inshore game fish are especially fond of them.

baby bluefish often provide forage for larger bluefish and other species. A modified Spread Fly like the one pictured on page 59 will serve very well.

We hope that this survey will help you sharpen your powers of observation regarding the naturals we, as fishermen, imitate. For further treatment of the subject, we recommend that you consult some of the following:

- Alan Caolo, *Fly Fisherman's Guide to Atlantic Baitfish & Other Food Sources,* Frank Amato Publications, 1995.
- A. J. McClane, *Field Guide to Saltwater Fishes of North America,* Henry Holt & Co., 1978.
- C. R. Robins and G. Carleton Ray, *Peterson Field Guide: Fishes of the Atlantic Coast,* Houghton Mifflin Co., 1986.
- George V. Roberts, Jr., *A Flyfisher's Guide to Salt Water Naturals and Their Imitations,* Ragged Mountain Press, 1994.
- Lou Tabory, *Guide to Saltwater Baits,* Lyons and Burford, 1995.

Chapter Two

Materials and Tools

Not so many years ago, there were far fewer fly shops than there now are and virtually no shops specializing in saltwater flies. Freshwater materials had to be adapted, and good hooks were few, both in terms of availability and style. We recall, too, when dyed materials were considered sacrilege: "It must be tied with natural blue dun and nothing else." Browse through any fly-tying catalogue or visit a local fly shop today, and you will immediately be struck by the wide range of materials and tools now available. We don't limit our thinking when it comes to materials selection. We're always on the lookout for new items that will meet our needs. There follows a sampling of some of the most common materials and tools we employ when creating Pop Fleyes, along with comments about using them. Nearly all the natural and synthetic products are available in a wide range of colors. In no way are we attempting to cover the broad spectrum of available tying paraphernalia or being dogmatic about material and tool selection. Although these comments and recommendations represent extensive trial and error, if you have had better results with another material, feel free to use that. We are always on the lookout for new products, too. We are especially thankful to the many suppliers of tying materials, especially manufacturers of synthetics who have been responsive to the needs of fly tiers. Their products make what we do possible.

MATERIALS

Natural Hairs and Feathers

Bucktail. This deer hair is one of our most widely used natural materials. We use it in all lengths, colors, and textures, generally preferring a moderate crinkle. It is rel-

Assorted bucktails. This is one of the most commonly used of all materials.

Saddle pads and strung hackles.

atively inexpensive, and its durability, buoyancy, and the taper of the hairs make it ideal for many purposes. Most of the usable hair is toward the top. The closer you move to the base, the more the hair tends to be hollow and flare when tied down.

Saddle Hackles. We use both long, thin, sleek hackles and wide, webby ones, each for different fly requirements. If you purchase a saddle pad—feathers on the skin—you will get a range of sizes but fewer of any given size. You can purchase "strung" saddle hackles, which are sorted and sized, and get a large number of one size. It's good to use both, since you don't want to waste your longest hackles on small flies.

Sheep Fleece, or Ram's Wool. We consider this an important material. We use a lot of this for Siliclones, as well as facing for Large Cotton Candies or other flies. It's the material called for when fashioning the front end of a Woolhead Sculpin. Select fleece that is fluffy in texture, not cottony, which packs too densely. Unfortunately, many tiers have yet to discover the advantages of fleece, and therefore, many fly shops do not carry a good selection.

Other Materials. Marabou, ostrich herl, peacock herl, and a few other traditional feathers have application for some Pop Fleye patterns and will be noted in the step-by-step instructions.

Sheep fleece.

Synthetic Hairs and Fibers

The market is flooded with synthetics, and each year new ones evolve, some adopted from other industries and some developed specifically for fly tying. Here are some of those we have found particularly suited to our flies.

Super Hair and UltraHair. These two similar materials are perhaps among the most widely used synthetics for our flies. We strongly prefer the more translucent over the opaque colors, preferring greens, tans, blues, grays, and polar bear white. Like most synthetics, these are not tapered, but you can effect nice, tapered lines in

Super Hair is long, translucent, and durable.

Use a hair dryer and comb to straighten nylon hairs.

your flies with judicious scissor work. See the instructions for Surf Candies in the next chapter.

These fibers are nylon and will take a set if left curled or bent, which often happens when they are left in a drawer for any length of time. We have tried many ways to straighten the fibers and found that the best employs an electric hair dryer. Use the high setting. Hold the hair in one hand in front of the stream of air, and repeatedly stroke the fibers with an antistatic comb. The heat appears to soften the material just slightly, so that the kinks and curls disappear in short order when combed. You can custom-blend colors by rolling small bunches of different colors back and forth between the index finger and thumb of one hand while combing the fibers with the comb held in your other hand. Remember that if you use more than one color hair, use less of each, or else you will have great difficulty in making lightly dressed fly. We once had a tier in class wonder how he could tie a trim Mickey Finn streamer if he had to use three colors of bucktail for the wing, yellow topped by red, topped by yellow. When we suggested he use only one-third as much for each color, his face lit up as if he had just learned the riddle of the Sphinx. Sometimes the obvious isn't so obvious.

Bozo Hair and Kinky Fiber. These and several similar synthetics are excellent for making large flies. Use thinning scissors (see below) for shaping and trimming these fibers. They have lively texture, and we find they don't cling together, mat, or tangle as some other products do. They are lightweight, easy to work with, and don't absorb water. When cast, they shed most of the water, making flies lighter and casting easier. Kinky Fiber is also available premixed with Angel Hair tinsel for exceptionally lifelike fly texture.

Big Fly Fiber. We use this for our largest flies. You can trim the teased, kinky portion at the front end of these fibers to make a fly that is less full, or trim the straight fibers at the rear to control the length. See the final chapter on using successive bunches of Big Fly Fiber for really huge creations.

Bozo Hair is used for large flies like the Cotton Candy.

Big Fly Fiber is used for the largest Pop Fleyes.

Polafibre and Craft Fur. These two soft, opaque synthetics, shorter in length than any of the above, are ideally suited to smaller flies. Both have good sheen and are easy to work with.

Sililegs. You can incorporate these soft, flexible rubber-band-style legs into shrimp, squid, crab, and other such imitations.

Flash

We use this general term to indicate all tinsel-type materials, metallic, mylar, holographics, and other materials that are used to add flash or sparkle to flies. Try different ones with your flies; different types of flash will produce different effects in the water. Silver is by far the most used, but often gold, pearl, or some rainbow blends complement a pattern well. As a rule, flies require less flash than anglers imagine. More subtle suggestions are generally more effective than large concentrations of flash material.

Flashabou. This is one of the first of the modern limp, nontarnishing tinsels, and it's still our all-around favorite. Lefty Kreh gave us this tip: Since most of the flash occurs near the ends of the strips as they flutter, cut the ends different lengths for better flash. You can also produce a slightly different flash effect by pulling the last half inch or so of Flashbou strips between your thumb and the back edge of a scissor blade, which will curl the ends of the tinsel, like curling ribbon used in gift wrapping. Silver and pearlescent are most useful, although it is available in a rainbow of colors. We generally use the standard width, but it's also available in a wider, saltwater version.

Krystal Flash. Tightly twisted Flashabou, Krystal Flash has a little more body and gives off more subtle reflectance. Both Krystal Flash and Flashabou give added enhancement to flies if left extending 1/4 inch or so beyond the end of the other materials.

Sparkleflash, Polar Flash, and Ragged Edge. Each of these, like the above products, gives a slightly different flash effect. All are good materials, but since they each complement different flies in different ways, in specific instances we prefer one over another.

(Left to right) Krystal Flash, Flashabou, Sparkleflash, Fluorofibre, and Estaz.

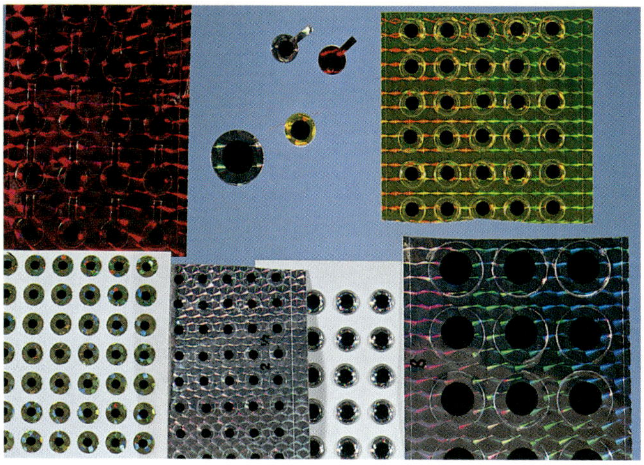

An assortment of prism eyes.

Angel Hair. This fine tinsel material, like cotton candy, gives subtle flash and is easy to use. Just pull out a tuft, tie it down, and trim away the excess.

Braided Mylar Piping. Available in different colors and sizes. You can wrap piping around a hook, like chenille or floss, or slip it over a strand of monofilament to fashion a body extension and imitate the silver stripe common to many baitfish. Pull the twisted cotton core from the piping before using it.

Estaz and Cactus Chenille. These strands are easy to wrap around a fly body and are a quick way to add sparkle and texture to flies. Cactus Chenille is somewhat bushier and larger in diameter.

Comes Alive. This adds effective, scalelike sparkle with pearlescence.

Fluorofibre. A few fibers will add wonderful fluorescence or iridescence, which appears to make flies light up. We find the pearl color very useful. A tuft of hot orange or red makes a colorful and attractive throat or gill representation.

Prism Eyes. We believe that eyes are important for most patterns, but they should be easy to attach and not add weight. Witchcraft Tape Products and other companies manufacture adhesive-backed, self-sticking prism eyes. A spot of cyanoacrylate or other glue assures that they won't come off your flies readily. Some now have a small tab that you can tie down with your thread for added security. Some patterns are more effective when they incorporate the more bulging effect of 3D eyes (see lower center of photo). All these come in a variety of sizes and colors. Silver iris with black pupil is the most realistic and most used. You can also change the iris color of the silver eyes with a red, green, or yellow marking pen. Here's an important tip. Especially when attaching prism eyes to epoxy or silicone flies, crease them sharply through their center before peeling them from the paper.

Crease prism eyes before attaching them, so that they will conform to the contour of your flies.

This gives them a curvature, so that they mold to the contour of your flies. Unless you do this, instead of clinging, they will spring straight and stand out like hubcaps along the sides of your flies.

Thread

Clear Monofilament Thread. Phil Camera, of Larva Lace, first put us on to the idea of tying with mono thread, and all the flies in this book, except Bob's Banger, were tied with fine Larva Lace clear monofilament thread. Gudebrod and Danville also make similar threads, and both are excellent. Mono thread allows the color of the materials underneath to show through, and relying on one type obviates the need for storing a variety of colors. Of course, you should tie with whatever thread you prefer and are most comfortable using.

Beads and Cones

Some of the most popular and widely used Pop Fleyes, like the Jiggy and its variations, employ cone heads. Another, the Deep Candy, has a large bead head. We use

(Clockwise from left) Cone heads, beads, Jiggy heads.

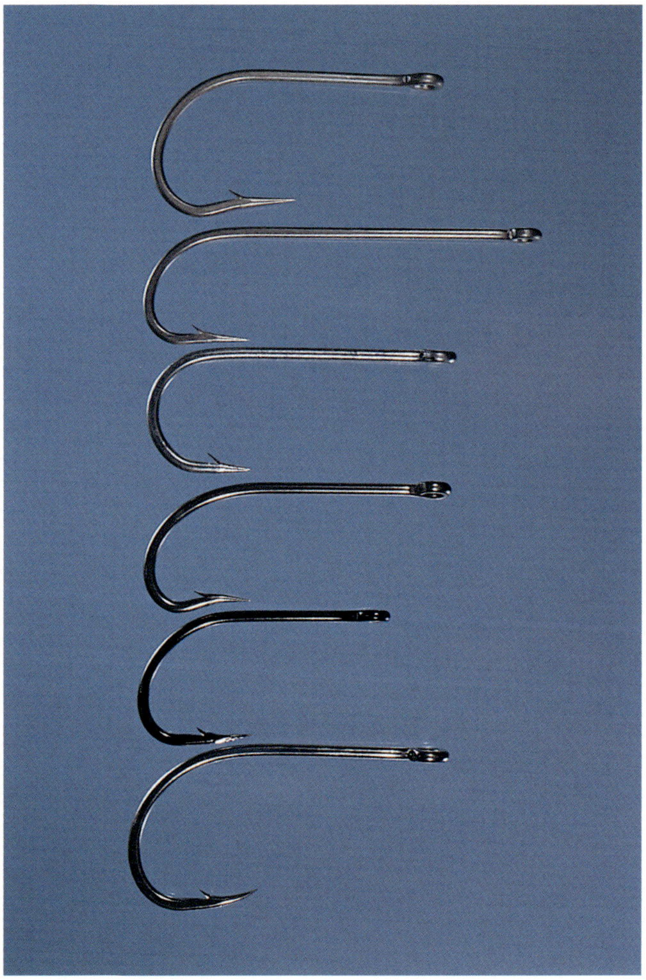

Some favorite hooks: (top to bottom) Tiemco 800S, Tiemco 900S, Partridge Homosassa Special, Partridge Sea Prince, Owner AKI, Trey Combs.

lead or tungsten cone heads in silver, gold, or black finish. The weight at the front of a fly produces a good jigging motion and cannot be broken off by hitting rocks or other obstacles. For additional weight, you can use a larger-size cone; two cones, one facing forward and one to the rear; or a cone plus bead. Cones and beads are available from several manufacturers, and Jiggy Heads, specifically designed for Jiggies by Bob Popovics and Stu Dickens of Bestco Enterprises, are now available. They have recessed, flattened sides that readily accept prism eyes, larger holes for easier fit over hook barbs, and notches that allow them to be snugged up against the hook eye and resist turning. Their weight can be increased slightly by pushing a few turns of lead wire into the hollowed-out center cavity (see Jiggy instructions, page 52.)

Hooks

The hook is the most critical component of the fly. The hook selected should complement the fly design, and it should not straighten, bend, break, or dull in the heat of battle. Poor hooks have let us down more often than rod, reel, or leader failures. We prefer stainless steel, and we crush the barbs, believing they penetrate more readily, cause less damage to fish, and are safer for anglers. We also search for hooks that will fit the design of the fly we are tying. For example, the Jiggy became a viable design with the introduction of the Tiemco 911S hook; it has the ideal length, bend, weight, and strength. The Siliclone ties best on a shorter shank with a wider, round bend, large gape, and heavy wire. We found the Partridge Homosassa hook ideal for it, although the point doesn't hold up as well as some other hooks. The Trey Combs and Owner AKI hooks are perfect large flies like Cotton Candies. Sizes between 2 and 4/0 are the most widely used, though some flies call for larger or smaller.

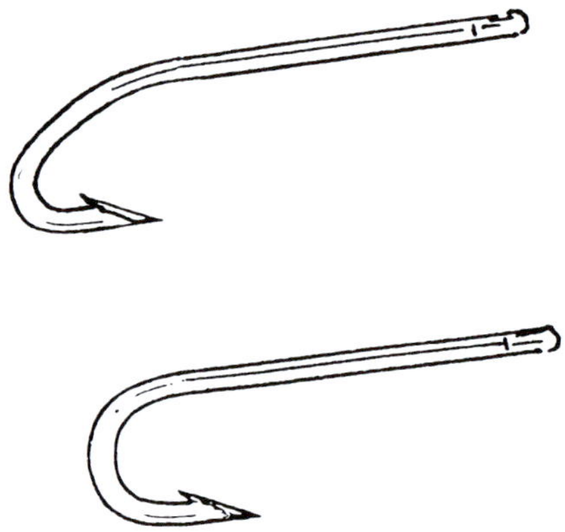

Different bends and shank lengths are better suited to different flies. Use hooks that complement your fly design.

The wrong hook selection for a particular fly can result in a fly that fouls when cast.

Glues and Cements

Cyanoacrylate. Marketed by various manufacturers under different names, including Krazy Glue, Zap-A-Gap, and Fishin' Glue, cyanoacrylate (CA) has many incidental uses in tying, which we will mention at times in the tying instructions. It sometimes helps to use an accelerator, or kicker, with CA. Just spritz a little of the accelerator onto the glue and it hardens instantly. Exercise caution when using this material; it can quickly bond fingers. And, as with all chemical substances, read warning labels, use them in ventilated areas, and be aware of possible allergic reactions.

An assortment of useful glues and cements.

Flexament. This head cement saturates threads well. Occasionally you may have to thin it out with Flexament thinner.

Hard as Nails. Available at cosmetic counters, this is another good, all-purpose head cement. We like to use this one to restore epoxy flies that have had encounters with toothy fish. There are many other excellent head cements on the market as well.

Flex Loc. A spectator at a recent fly-fishing show put us on to this new Larva Lace product. With your fingertip, rub a little lightly over the hairs of Cotton Candies, 3Ds, or similar flies. It helps hold a fly's form and shape without matting and gluing the fibers together. They stay soft, flexible, and apart. It dries instantly and doesn't discolor the fibers.

Some nontoxic products.

Soft Body. This rubbery substance is claimed to be nontoxic and is available in thin or thick consistency. You can use it to coat the heads and wraps of many flies. It doesn't replace epoxy but can be used as an alternative, especially for Jiggies (see page 47), when you are in a hurry or don't require the extra durability of epoxy. It's also less messy; just dip the head of the finished fly into the Soft Body and put it onto a rotating drying wheel.

Hard Head. Another nontoxic product. A water-base, polyurethane formula that we find useful for coating thread wraps, it has good consistency, and stays where it's put, and has surprising durability. We feel that environmentally safe products have an important role in our sport and encourage manufacturers to create more and fishermen to use them.

Epoxy and Silicone. These two materials are much identified with Pop Fleyes. They will be treated in more detail in the appropriate chapters under those titles.

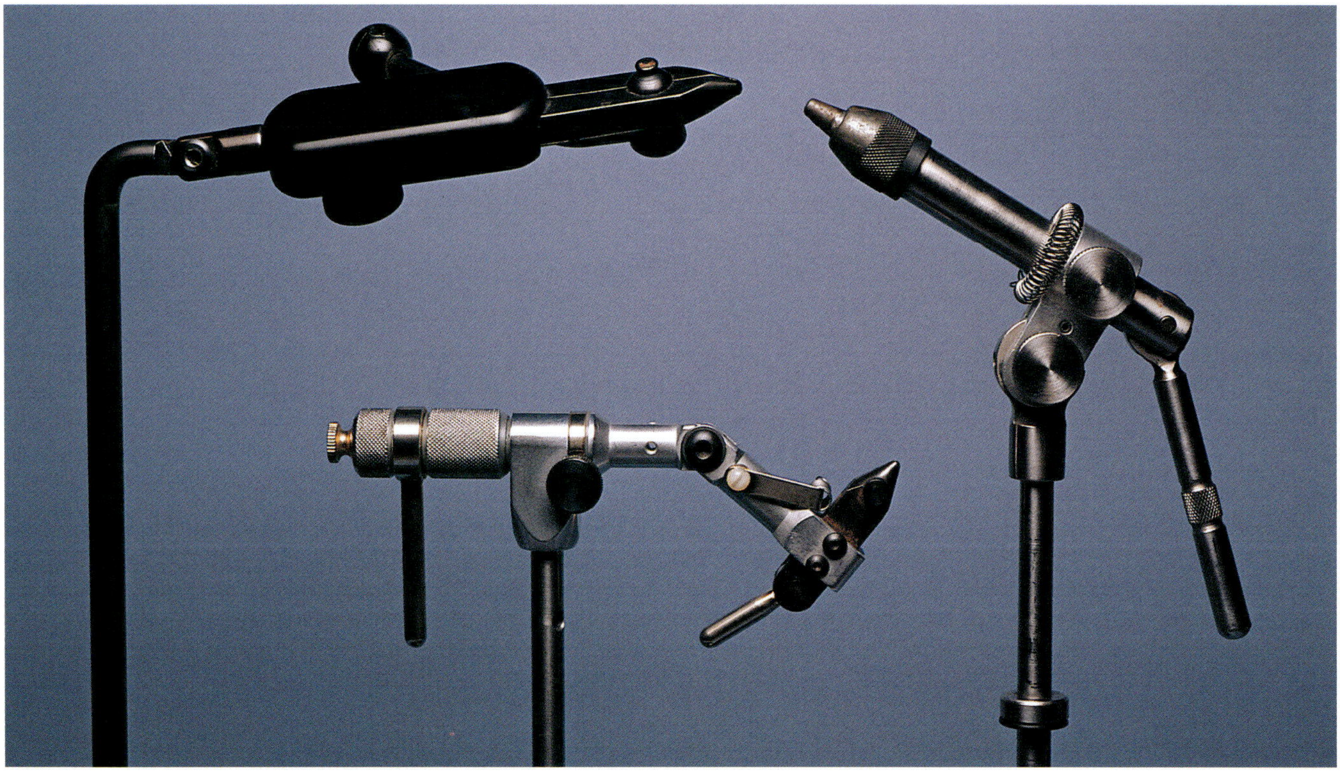

(Left to right) Regal, Renzetti (our favorite), and Dyna-King are all good saltwater vises.

TOOLS

Vise. Strong gripping power, especially for large saltwater hooks is the first requirement. Any vise that has that quality will suffice. Some vises that work well for trout flies may not pass muster when subjected to the size and leverage of large, long hooks. We have even had several vises explode when subjected to the pressures of holding large hooks, either because of poor design or defective parts. The jaws of any vise you are considering should open to accept at least a 5/0 hook. Regal, Dyna-King, HMH, and several top-line manufacturers make vises adequate for the demands of saltwater work. A rotating vise has decided advantages over a stationary vise or one with limited movements. Our first choice by a wide margin, for all our tying, is the Renzetti top-of-the-line Master's Vise. The Renzetti is the standard by which others are judged, and several makers have tried to copy its features. It has great gripping power, a number of precise adjustments, and full 360-degree rotation, which is a distinct advantage for examining flies and working, getting materials even, and applying lacquer and epoxy. A host of accessories are available, from bobbin cradle to high-speed winding crank. A Salt Water Traveler model is also now available. It has the most important features of the Master's Vise at a more economical price. Whatever vise you select, you have the option of mounting it with a C-clamp at the edge of the table or using a pedestal base. We prefer the latter, which allows us to sit closer to the table and rest our arms on the surface.

Combs and Brushes. Some of the materials we use must be brushed or combed to make them more manageable or remove tangles or knots. A wire dog brush for wool fleece and an antistatic bone comb or mustache comb for nylon hairs are indispensable.

Scissors. You will want different scissors for different cutting needs: a pair of fine-point, surgical iris scissors for delicate work, a pair of thinning scissors for shaping hairs like Bozo Hair and Kinky Fiber, plus a pair with at least one serrated-edge blade. Whether you use curved or straight blades is largely a matter of personal preference, but make sure the loops are large enough for your fingers to slip in and out easily. For cutting hairs, especially some of the synthetics, the serrated-edge scissors are necessary. They hold the material in place so it doesn't slip when you are trying to cut it.

Bobbin. A bobbin, or spool holder, with ceramic tube, or at least a ceramic ring at the end of the tube, will last longer and not fray or cut thread. They are available in regular or heavy-duty models. Either will work fine.

Bodkin. Also known as a dubbing needle, a bodkin is indispensable. More than just an instrument for applying head cement, it is the primary tool for sculpting epoxy bodies and straightening hair and fleece tangles. These uses will be discussed in the appropriate tying sections.

A wire dog brush and antistatic bone comb are essential tying aids.

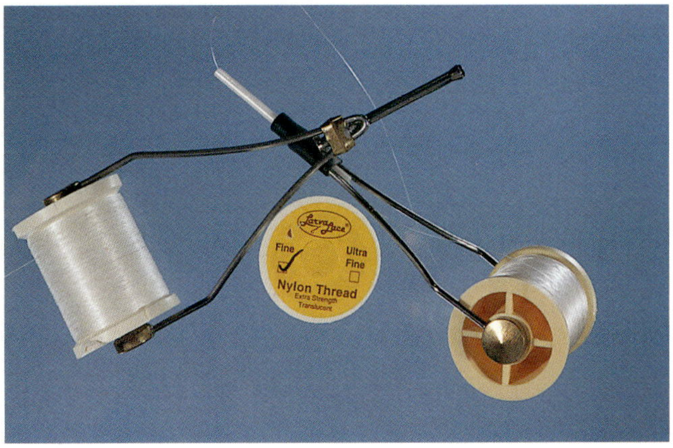

Ceramic bobbins help prevent monofilament thread breakage.

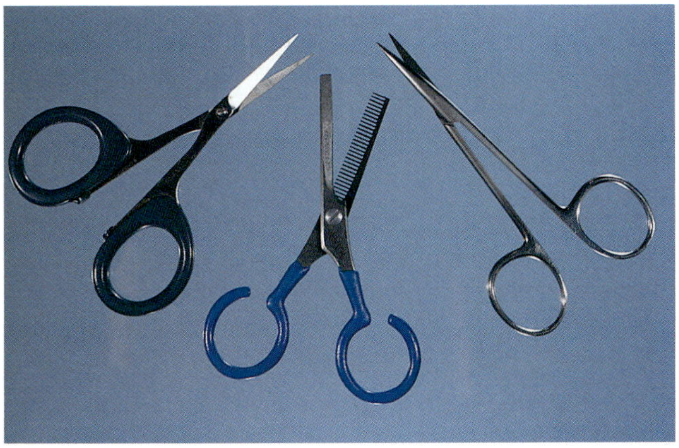

(Left to right) Straight blade, thinning, and curved fine-point scissors all have uses.

An electric drying-curing wheel facilitates the making of certain epoxy flies.

Scissors with serrated-edge blades facilitate cutting slick synthetic hairs.

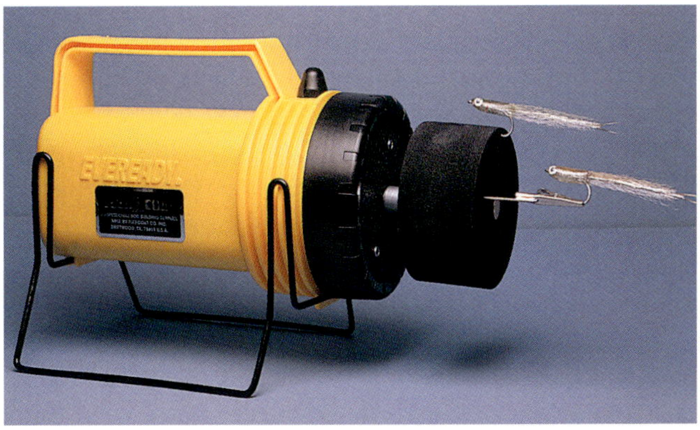

Battery operated portable drying wheel by Flexcoat.

Drying Wheel. For some epoxy flies, a rotating drying or curing wheel can be a great convenience, even though using one is not vital. A small, low-speed rotisserie motor like those used for rod dryers is perfect for fly tying. You can make your own, like the one shown here from components purchased from rod-building supply houses or electronics stores. Flexcoat Company makes the handy battery operated portable dryer also shown here.

Note: Many tiers believe a rotary dryer is essential and more efficient than hand manipulation and insist on using it for epoxy flies. We disagree and do not use a

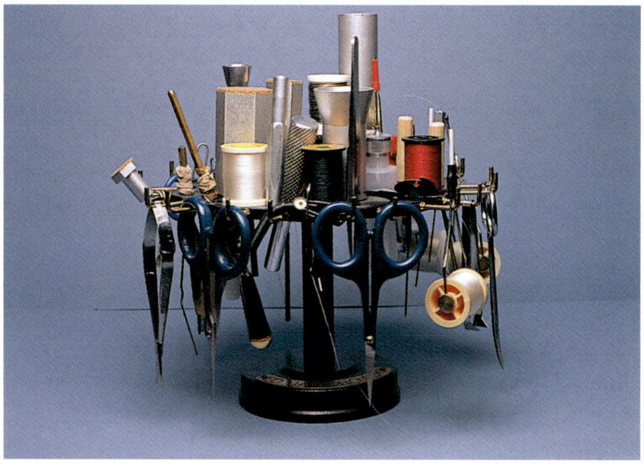

Mick Summerfield of England designed this rotating tool caddy that turns on ball bearings.

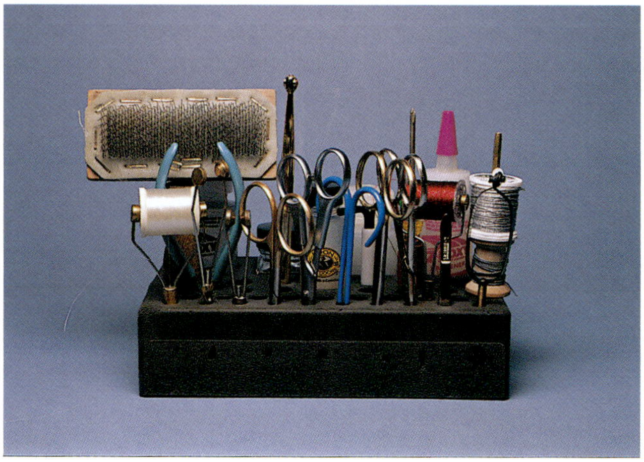

Renzetti tool caddy.

A handy tinsel rack made by noted photographer-angler Irv Swope.

wheel for most of our patterns, other than to allow additional curing time once the epoxy has gelled. We feel strongly that hand turning and manipulating the epoxy with a bodkin is the key to mastering epoxy fly design. If you want anything but a cylindrical or football-shaped body, you should manipulate by hand. One of the problems is that the wheel rotates at a constant rate, while the epoxy is drying at a variable rate, so it is nearly impossible to produce fly body shapes other than rounded cross sections. Some Surf Candy variations, the Diet Candy, Ultra Shrimp, Spread Fly, 'Cuda Candy, and Keel Eel simply cannot be made with a wheel. We do, however, use a drying wheel for Jiggies and variations of Surf Candies that do not call for a sculpted or modeled body.

Racks and Caddies. You can fashion a homemade rack or caddy to hold your fly-tying tools or purchase one of the commercial models on the market. The important point is to make your tying time efficient and pleasurable. It won't be if you have to chase down tools

John Zajano made this fly-drying rack for us, after the original by Irv Swope.

that roll off the table or constantly get mislaid. A simple wire rack keeps tinsels and other hanging materials straight, organized, and handy. Once you've applied epoxy

Permanent markers have a variety of uses for the saltwater tier.

or head cement to your flies, it's a good idea to place them into some sort of drying rack or hang them until they are fully dry. Noted angler-photographer Irv Swope fashioned various fly-drying racks, tinsel racks, and other assorted fly-tying accessories.

Marking Pens. Sharpie, Pantone, and other manufacturers sell permanent marking pens that have a variety of uses in fly tying, such as adding gills, body markings, and producing two-tone effects.

A fly-tying area should have everything in easy reach.

SETTING UP A TYING AREA

A tying light and a magnifier are accessories that will help you to produce better results. The excellent Giraffe Lighting and Magnifying System, by Goodwin Mfg., is used in the accompanying photo, although others are available, some portable enough for traveling. Most lights designed for this purpose have a high-intensity bulb. Make certain that it is shielded or aimed so that it doesn't shine directly toward your eyes when working. Note that the vise is fitted into a base attached to the table, through which a hole can be drilled. The tool caddy and drying wheel, plus the large hook file system on the table to the right and the materials drawers in the rear, are all close at hand for the tier. Spend some time in selecting the right chair. Sitting for long periods of time in an uncomfortable chair will likely discourage you from spending much time at the vise.

Chapter Three

Epoxy Pop Fleyes

WORKING WITH EPOXY

Epoxy Pop Fleyes have given a wholly new direction to saltwater tying. Epoxy is one of the most widely used synthetic materials for saltwater flies today, whether for protecting wraps or providing form for fly bodies. While epoxy is available in colors, colorless or clear is generally the most useful. It consists of two chemicals, an epoxy resin and a hardener. When the two are mixed, a chemical reaction causes the material to harden. You can purchase the sets in one-ounce, parallel syringe tubes, which, when squeezed, force out equal amounts of the two chemicals. Six-ounce plastic bottles are more economical if you plan to use larger amounts. Whichever package you use, it's critical to keep the proportions equal if the material is to harden properly. We strongly suggest that you begin by practicing with epoxy on a bare hook, to get a sense of the way it flows and how to achieve different shapes using simply your bodkin during different stages of the hardening process.

We prefer Devcon brand clear, five-minute epoxy, the most useful for most purposes, although other brands we have tried work well also. With this, you have about

LEFTY KREH

four minutes actual working time. Sometimes thirty-minute epoxy is desirable, especially when making flies that don't require hand sculpting and can be put immediately on a drying wheel. As a rule, the longer the material takes to cure, the less yellowing you are likely to experience, although nearly all epoxies yellow with time. More importantly, perhaps, you gain more working time. With the five-minute type, you can only get a few flies—perhaps six Jiggies—done before the material sets. It's then necessary to mix up successive batches of the epoxy. Using the thirty-minute type and putting the flies on a drying wheel, you can prepare two or three times as many flies per batch of epoxy, since the working time is about ten minutes before it begins thickening. Incidentally, one-minute hardening epoxies have their place in certain tying operations, but generally speaking, we have found that the short working time, until it gets gummy and stops flowing, allows us too little opportunity to manipulate the material and form many of our flies. It simply sets too fast for most of the work we do, and we don't recommend it for new users.

It's a good idea to do all your tying at one time and then apply the epoxy coating closer to the time you will use the flies. This minimizes yellowing of flies that sit in fly boxes for months or years after tying. Exposure to strong sunlight appears to greatly hasten the yellowing process. We left flies in direct sunlight, and they turned brown in a few days. In sealed frames and out of the light, they take far longer to turn. If your flies are exposed to the sun, as when rigged and ready on your boat or truck, protect them with a cover that snaps over the fly. Such fly and lure holders are available in many tackle shops and are designed to protect anglers from exposed hooks.

If you want a body that is not perfectly round in cross section, don't put it into a drying wheel until you have shaped the body to your satisfaction and are certain that the epoxy has stopped flowing. If you place the fly into the wheel too soon—that is, while the epoxy is still quite liquid—the epoxy will redistribute itself, and the fly will probably turn out round. If you put it on while there is still a little movement to the epoxy, it may well move just a bit and turn out lopsided or misformed. Keep in mind, too, that although the hardening time may be listed as one, five, or thirty minutes, it may take an hour or more before the substance is fully cured and hard. Note the neatly formed noses of the Surf Candies in the photo on page 33, which are meant to simulate bay anchovies, or the Keel Eel on page 46. The hair on the top of the nose is folded back to imitate their rounded snouts. This fine touch can be done only by turning the fly by hand until the epoxy sets. On a wheel, the epoxy would have shifted the shape.

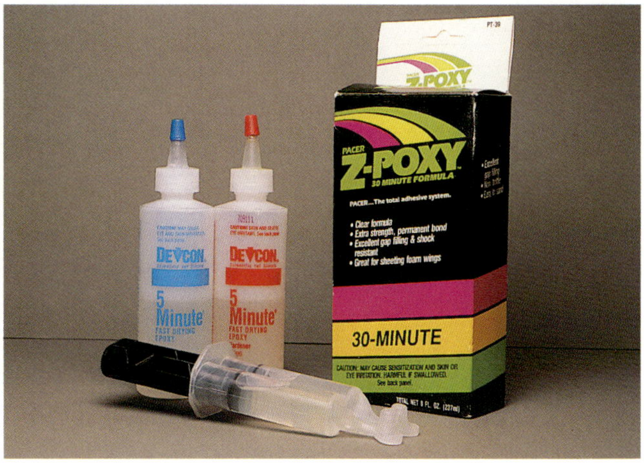

Various types of epoxy.

Uneven or disproportionate mixing of the two components may leave the epoxy tacky for an inordinate time. If this should happen, simply coat the epoxy with Hard as Nails clear nail polish. When it dries, the fly body will be smooth and hard. Incidentally, the same remedy will restore to near-new condition flies that have been chewed by fish.

We find it convenient to squeeze the epoxy onto small Post-It or similar self-sticking note sheets, which are available from any stationery store. They are inexpensive, convenient, and stay put while you are working the epoxy, and you can simply throw them away when finished, making cleanup easy. Make it a habit to follow the same procedure when squeezing out the epoxy—that is, either the resin bead first or the hardener. The only reason being that if you get distracted from your tying before finishing the epoxy chore, you will know what the bead on the paper is. (We've gotten confused at times.) Some tiers claim that mixing epoxy with a wooden implement, like a popsicle stick or toothpick, will hasten yellowing. This has not been our experience. Nor will the yellow paper we use hasten yellowing.

When mixing the two chemicals, use your dubbing needle, but don't stir aggressively, as this can cause bubbles to form in the mixture. Rather, gently swirl and fold them in the way you mix cake batter.

Avoid a very cool environment. Epoxy mixes and works better when the air is slightly warmer. Exposing the mixed epoxy briefly to the heat of your tying lamp will make it flow better and help eliminate bubbles. You can stop manipulating the fly once the epoxy starts to harden. Test it on the mixing pad, not on the fly itself, by cross stroking the epoxy with your bodkin, making an X or tic-tac-toe design. If it flows back and the scores you made with your bodkin fill in, keep rotating the fly. You know the epoxy on your fly is starting to gel when the bead on the paper has stopped flowing and is now

Measure beads of epoxy and hardener prior to mixing.

Stir and fold epoxy with a bodkin.

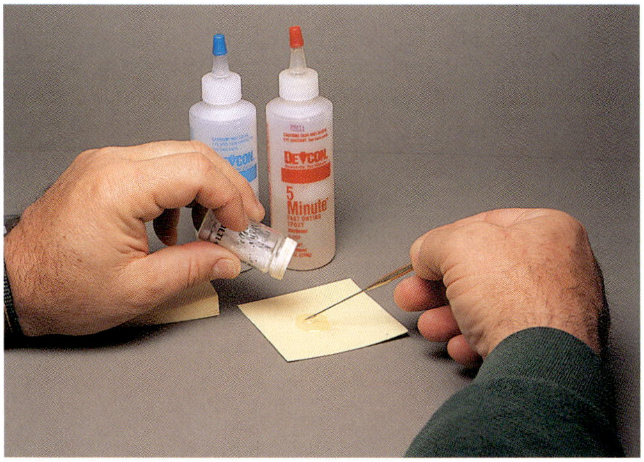

Sprinkle glitter into the mixed epoxy for scalelike sparkle.

This handy gadget cleans epoxy from your bodkin.

hardening. You can add glitter to the epoxy for scalelike effects by sprinkling glitter powder (available at most craft shops) into the epoxy while you mix it. As an alternative, though not so convenient, you can cut up mylar, tinsel, Flashabou, or other flash material into very fine pieces and mix that into the epoxy as you stir it. You can also add a drop or two of food coloring for creative color effects.

Tier Edie Mashiko gave us a great idea for keeping our bodkin clean and free of hardened epoxy. Stuff some copper scrubber material into an empty plastic film canister and poke a small hole in the lid. When finished with your epoxy chores, just shove the bodkin through the hole, and the needle will always be clean and ready to use.

Caution: Most importantly, when working with epoxy or any other chemicals, such as silicone, which is discussed in the next chapter, don't sit in a confined area. *Always work in a well-ventilated area, to avoid inhaling fumes, and follow cautions advised on the product labels.*

Surf Candies designed to simulate bay anchovies.

SURF CANDIES

We thought it fitting to begin our tying instructions with the Pop Fleyes signature fly. The original epoxies were tied with primarily one thought in mind: durability. Fish with sharp teeth can make short work of feathers, hair, and tinsel. Tiers had for some time used epoxy in lieu of head cement to protect thread wraps and prevent flies from unraveling, but the epoxy here was used to shape and protect the entire body. Early versions, tied with bucktail or polar bear hair (the latter now nearly impossible or illegal to procure) proved far less durable than the epoxy, so that the hair was often destroyed long before the body. After substituting several alternatives, we settled on UltraHair, manufactured by D. H. Thompson, and Super Hair, a similar material produced by Bestway Products. These synthetics were tougher than any natural fiber we tried. We have caught more than thirty bluefish on a single Candy, testifying to its near indestructibility.

Early in the evolution of these epoxy baitfish imitations, we began to appreciate added characteristics—namely, translucence, realism, flash, and weight. Mylar flash was first wrapped around the hook shank so it showed through the clear epoxy. We soon hit upon a strip of mylar piping over a piece of monofilament to simulate the bright lateral stripe and added a feather tail to simulate the black caudal outline of common baitfish. Instructions for what we now term a "full dress" Surf Candy are included below among the variations that we tie. Since we are always striving to make designs more tier friendly, we experimented with different ways to produce the flash effect. Currently, most of the basic Surf Candies we use are tied simply, as illustrated and discussed in detail below. You can add or adapt different components according to your need or whim, depending on your principal requirement, whether translucence, action, durability, or realism. For example, saddle

The Surf Candy redefined albacore and bonito fishing in the Northeast.

Tom Gilmore with a keen-eyed bonito that fell for an epoxy Surf Candy.

hackle points were added to the Bonito Candy to generate more tail action. Surf Candies have been modified in countless ways and renamed by countless tiers. They are among the most popular small baitfish imitations in use today for striped bass, bluefish, weakfish, false albacore, and bonito.

The following instructions and photos describe the procedures for creating most of the epoxy Pop Fleyes designs. In our instructions, we use the term "flash" generically, to indicate variously one of the tinsel-like materials such as Flashabou, Krystal Flash, Angel Hair, or similar products. Since we take the approach of modular construction in our fly tying, we readily mix and match various components. In the samples shown throughout this text, we are showing the range of possibilities by using different hairs and tinsels on different patterns. Feel free to use Super Hair, UltraHair, Craft Fur, bucktail, and so forth as the mood and your instincts direct you. You can, for example, add a bead or cone to the front of a Rabbit Candy or any other design. It is also difficult to give precise amounts of materials to use, as these will vary with the size of the hook and the bait being imitated. Likewise, colors provide many options. The sample flies tied here are not to be regarded as hard-and-fast dictates on any of these issues. They represent our thinking and our approach to problem solving in the creative tying process. Use the instructions and photos as a guide. We are specific when we need to be, and the text will indicate that. Otherwise, be creative, but always with a reason for any innovation.

Surf Candy

This is the way we tie most of the Candies we use. Since the Surf Candy was first introduced, tiers have experimented with other materials in place of the crinkled nylon fibers we like. Some use FisHair and many tiers like Craft Fur, which is soft, easy to work with, and makes it easy to get smooth bodies. Here's how to tie a basic Surf Candy, using Super Hair. We sometimes leave the hook shank bare, but tinsel or braid can be wrapped around the shank to add more interior flash.

Materials

Super Hair or UltraHair (you can also use Craft Fur, Kinky Fiber, another synthetic, or bucktail)
Standard or short shank saltwater hook, commonly #2 through 1/0; Tiemco 800S used here
Fine monofilament thread
Flashabou, Krystal Flash, or other preferred flash
Devcon clear five-minute epoxy
Self-sticking prism eyes
Red Sharpie permanent marker, fine or medium point

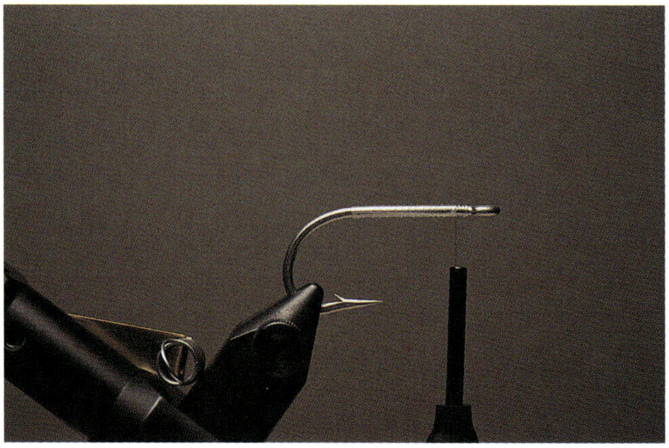

1. Wrap thread on the entire shank and leave it hanging close to the eye.

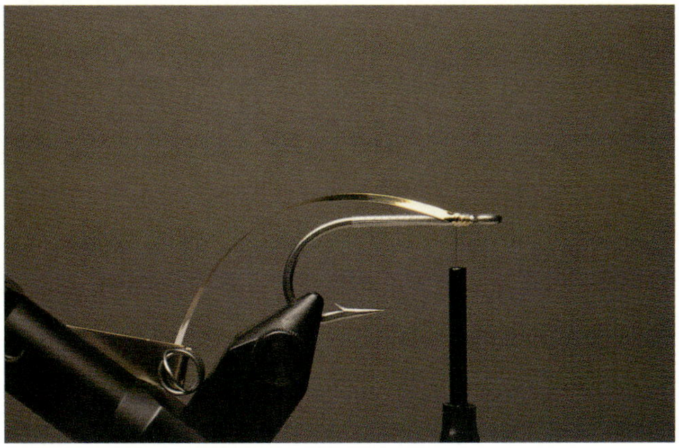

2. Attach mylar tinsel in front position.

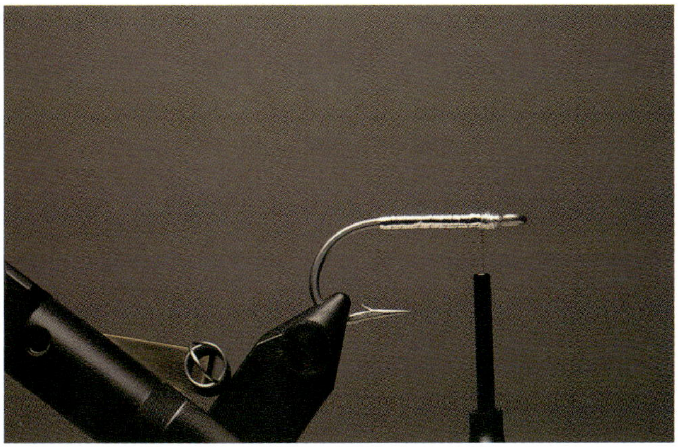

3. Wrap tinsel to the bend and back again to the front before tying off.

4. Tie in a bunch of UltraHair behind the hook eye on the top side of the shank. Before you attach it, trim the butt ends square, not tapered, and fasten it down only in the front of the fly, behind the eye. Don't fasten it securely yet. Note that the length is not critical when using synthetic hair, since this will be trimmed when the fly is completed. With bucktail or any natural hair, you will have to determine the finished length before you tie down the hair.

5. Using your index finger and thumb, spread the hair evenly around the hook shank, and then fasten it securely with tight wraps of thread.

6. Add some flash on the top and tie it down.

7. Prepare a second bunch of hair as above, and attach it to the top of the fly. This is normally in a contrasting color, but needn't be.

8. Prepare the five-minute epoxy by squeezing out a dime-size bead of each, epoxy resin and hardener. Mix as described earlier and apply using a bodkin. Make this first coat just heavy enough to avoid excessive sagging and dripping. This coat will determine the fly body thickness and shape. Start at the head and work gradually back to, but not beyond, the bend of the hook. Hold the wing material with the finger and thumb of your free hand, and force the epoxy in between the hairs so that they are saturated. Occasionally pull the hair into line to get a fuller or slimmer body, as you prefer, while the epoxy is setting. Finger pressure on the material is an important part of forming epoxy fly bodies. We recommend that you use a rotating drying wheel only if you want a round, cylindrical body. Otherwise, it's best to perform this operation with the hook in your hand or in a rotating vise so that you can control where you want the epoxy thicker or thinner, sculpting the body the whole time with your bodkin.

9. The first coat of epoxy has been applied. The shape and form of the fly are now determined. It is nearly always better to use two lighter coats than one heavy one. It's easier to work with thinner coats; you have less running and dripping problems, and the material cures better and more uniformly. Notice there are no uneven areas on the body. A material clip can be used to support the hair material. Keep the hair or fiber material parallel to the hook shank or just very slightly upward angled. If it is angled downward from the bend at all, it will impede the fly's action and movement.

10. After the epoxy is set and dry, apply small prism eyes. Before peeling them from their paper backing, sharply crease them, as shown on page 23, so that they will more closely follow the contour of the fly body and not stand out straight like car hubcaps.

11. The eyes in place, well forward on the head.

12. Red gill slashes can be added with a Sharpie marking pen. This is a simple and quick way to give a touch of realism. We have given up on any gill suggestions that involve additional tying steps.

13. Apply the second, finish epoxy coat.

14. If the epoxy runs or a drip forms, use your needle to reposition the epoxy, and keep rotating and turning the fly while you work with it. This coat will smooth out the finish and give a hard luster to the fly.

15. The completed Surf Candy, waiting to be trimmed.

16. Using the tips of your scissors, snip small amounts of material to get the shape you desire. Start near the hook bend and work to the rear. Don't just cut the tail square. Remember, most synthetics don't have a taper of their own, but you can make wonderful tapered flies with your scissor work.

17. The finished Surf Candy. (Actual size, $3\,^{1}/_{2}$ inches)

Fishing Tip: Wire Leaders

Surf Candies are durable, even when subjected to powerful bluefish teeth and jaws. Monofilament leaders, however, are vulnerable. Heavy monofilament bite, or shock, tippets have limits. First, the longer a truly large fish is on the line, the greater the odds are that it will eventually bite through the mono. Second, heavy mono inhibits fly action, especially when using smaller imitations like Surf Candies. We recommend single-strand, brown-colored, stainless steel trolling wire instead of monofilament or braided wire. No. 3, 4, or 5 wire works well, but it kinks readily. No. 9 or 10 wire seems heavy to anglers unaccustomed to using it, but it resists kinking and can be straightened easily if bent and will still perform well. Cut the wire in short traces, a foot or so in length. Make a Haywire Twist in the leader end and attach the other end to your fly with another Haywire. Some anglers like to use a snap here to facilitate fly changing. We simply cut the leader and fly off together and tie on another prewired fly. Fasten your tippet to the wire trace with your favorite clinch-type knot. If the wire bite tippet is limited to no more than about 4 inches, it will have no effect on casting and presentation. Incidentally, fish don't seem to shy from such short, heavy wire leaders. In fact, we have caught hundreds of striped bass while using them. For barracuda, you will need a longer wire trace, about 10 inches. In this case, we resort to flexible braided wire without nylon coating.

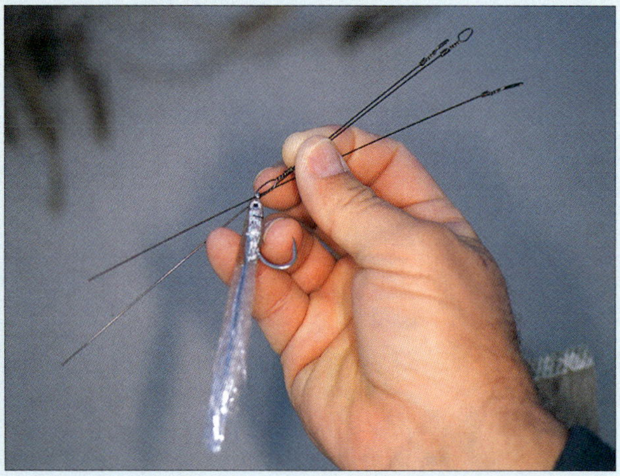

Ready and prerigged wire leaders.

Full Dress Surf Candy

We borrowed this term from the salmon fly tier's lexicon. Some baitfish, such as bay anchovies and silversides, sport a predominant, metallic-looking stripe the length of the body. This is one way to add that feature plus the tail. It may not be always necessary, but the technique adds realism when desired. Our underwater videos often indicate a dominant tail outline on baitfish. We recommend this exercise. Draw a fish tail and then lay a simple Surf Candy on top of it so the tail protrudes from the rear of the fly. You will immediately see the effect you can achieve by incorporating this into your fly.

Materials

Super Hair or UltraHair (you can also use Craft Fur, Kinky Fiber, another synthetic, or bucktail)
Standard or short shank saltwater hook, commonly #2 through 1/0; Tiemco 800S used here
Fine monofilament thread
Flashabou, Krystal Flash, or other preferred flash
Devcon clear five-minute epoxy
Self-sticking prism eyes
Short, stiff section of 20-pound monofilament
Fine braided silver piping
Section cut from saddle hackle, trimmed like a chevron, about 1/4 inch long

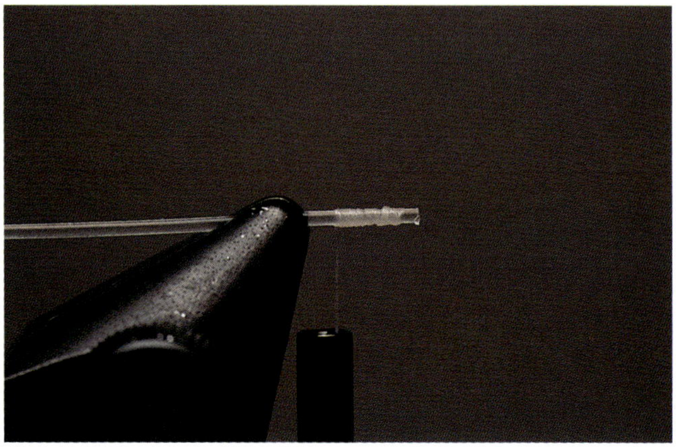

1. First prepare the tail by cutting a piece of stiff mono, about 20 pound-test, 3 1/2 inches long. Insert the mono in your vise so that only 1/4 inch protrudes. Crimping the end flat may help with your tying.

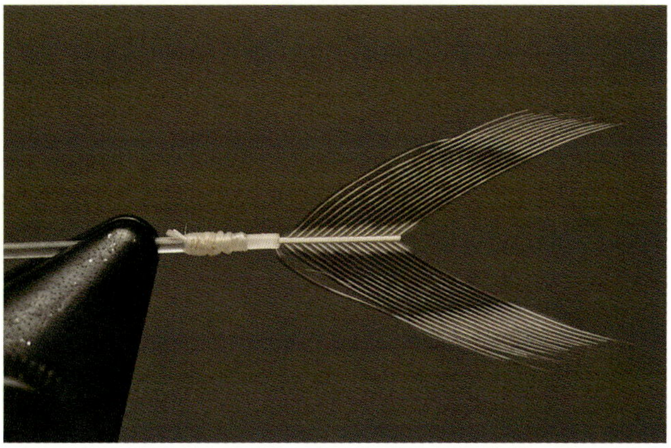

2. Cut a narrow section from a neck, flank, or saddle feather to the shape of a chevron to simulate the tail, with just a little stripped stem protruding. Tie the feather to the mono end.

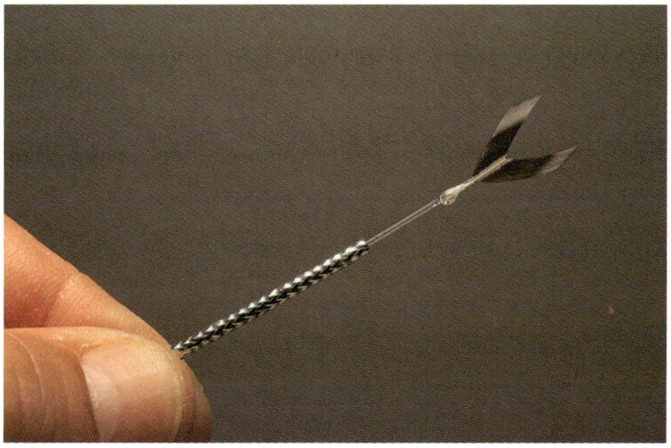

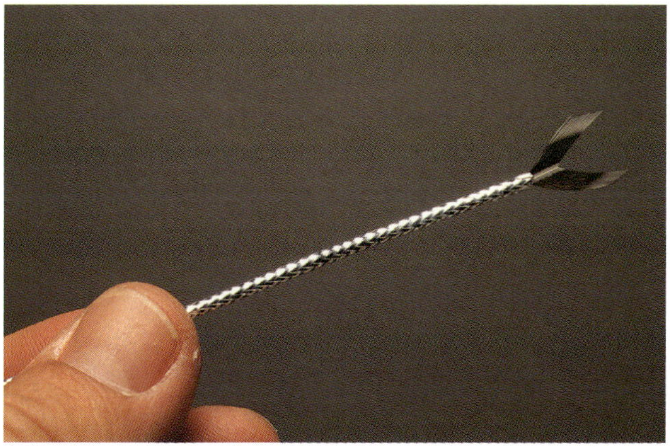

3. Remove the cotton core from a section of braided mylar piping. Insert the mono into the braided tube. A drop of cyanoacrylate (such as Krazy Glue) helps keep it in place. As an option, you can wrap the end of the braid with thread around the mono, and then push the mylar toward the tail so that it turns inside out to cover and protect the wraps and give a neater, more finished look. Some tiers dispense with the monofilament insertion in the braided tubing and insert hackle point feathers or a tuft of marabou directly into the braided tubing to simulate the tail. However, we have found that the mono insert strengthens that part of the fly and helps prevent shredding of the tinsel.

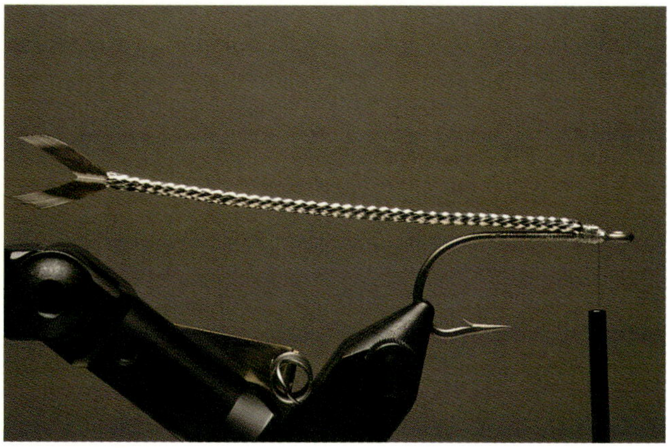

4. Attach the tail extension to the top of the hook shank, fastening it just behind the eye.

5. Complete the fly by applying the epoxy and eyes and trimming according to the instructions for the basic Surf Candy. To illustrate additional techniques, we have painted the belly with silver paint after the first coat of epoxy. We are here mimicking the belly sac of the Atlantic silversides, or spearing, shown in the baitfish section of the first chapter. (Actual size, 3 5/8 inches)

On the following pages are some additional variations on a theme. Using the Surf Candy procedures as a starting point, you can create other patterns simulating a variety of baitfish, shrimp, and even squid.

Diet Candy

This version suits fastidious fly tiers who enjoy more realism. When you put epoxy over the hair, the fibers will darken in color, so that the hair that protrudes to the rear on the back will be somewhat different in shade. By neatly trimming the hair short on top so it can't foul, and then covering only the belly portion of the fly with epoxy, you get a more natural coloration. Note that this is one of the many epoxy Pop Fleyes for which you can't use a rotating drying wheel.

Materials

Super Hair or UltraHair (you can also use Craft Fur, Kinky Fiber, another synthetic, or bucktail)
Standard or short shank saltwater hook, commonly #2 through 1/0; Tiemco 800S used here
Fine monofilament thread
Flashabou, Krystal Flash, or other preferred flash
Devcon clear five-minute epoxy
Self-sticking prism eyes
Straight strips of mylar flash in place of Flashabou or Krystal Flash

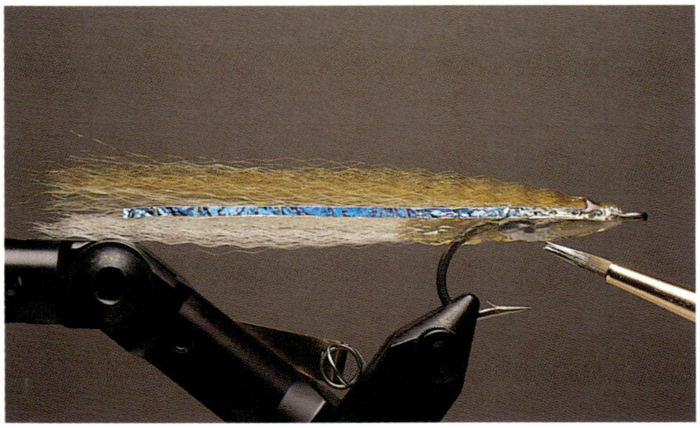

1. Attach hair as for the simple Surf Candy, but apply epoxy to the belly and only the top of the head wraps. When hard, paint the belly with silver paint.

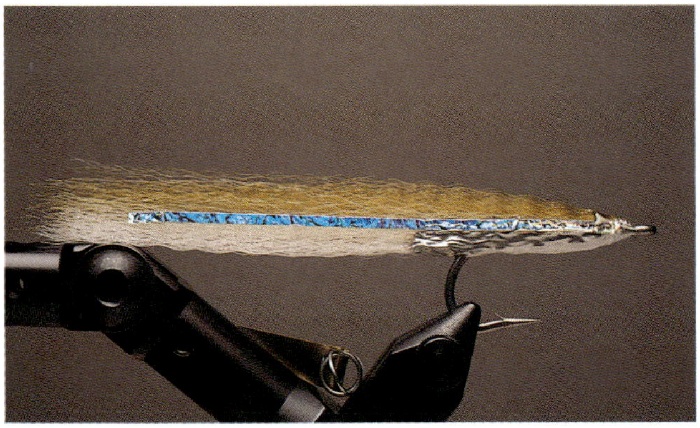

2. The belly painting is finished.

3. The finished and trimmed fly, complete with the second epoxy coat and eyes. Note the taper and short hairs on top, which prevent fouling. You can also add a tail assembly like that described for the Full Dress Surf Candy.

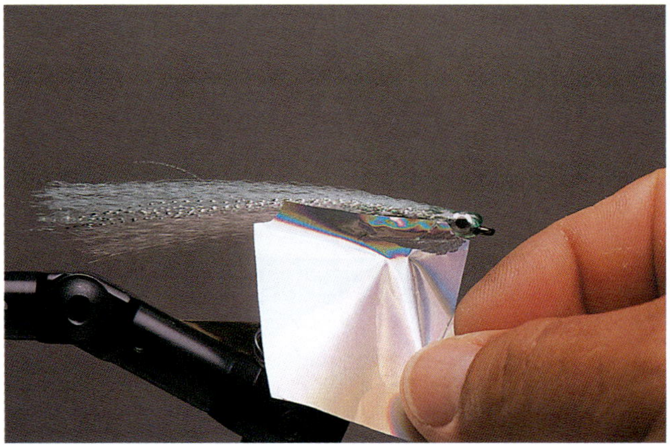

An option for the belly is to press silver transfer tape onto the finished fly belly and peel it away. The silver foil leaves a smooth, chrome-like finish. Or, use a Krylon silver leaf pen for a similar effect. (Actual size, 3 5/8 inches)

Fishing Tip: Picking Up Weighted Flies

Flies with concentrated weight, like Deep Candies, Jiggies, and Clouser Minnows, cause casting difficulties for some anglers. The problem usually has to do with getting the fly out of the water and moving smoothly at the start of the cast. The solution is to use a *roll-cast pickup.* Strip in the line, but don't pause to let the heavy fly sink. Simply make a roll cast so that the fly comes out of the water and turns over onto the surface. With practice, you will be able to shoot a little extra line on your roll cast. Now that you have the fly at the surface, and before it can sink again, immediately make your normal backcast and forward cast. The whole maneuver will work better if you bring your rod and arm well to the rear when you begin, and use longer strokes for the roll cast, backcast, and forward cast.

Roll cast a sinking fly or sinking line to the surface before executing a normal backcast.

Deep Candy

Undulating or jigging lure motions can be deadly, as the Clouser Deep Minnow has so effectively proven. By weighting the front end of a Surf Candy with a lead or tungsten bead, you can get the fly down better and produce a different action. The trick here is to avoid any gap behind the bead head.

Materials

Super Hair or UltraHair (you can also use Craft Fur, Kinky Fiber, another synthetic, or bucktail)
Standard or short shank saltwater hook, commonly #2 through 1/0; Tiemco 800S used here
Fine monofilament thread
Flashabou, Krystal Flash, or other preferred flash
Devcon clear five-minute epoxy
Self-sticking prism eyes
Silver- or gold-colored bead

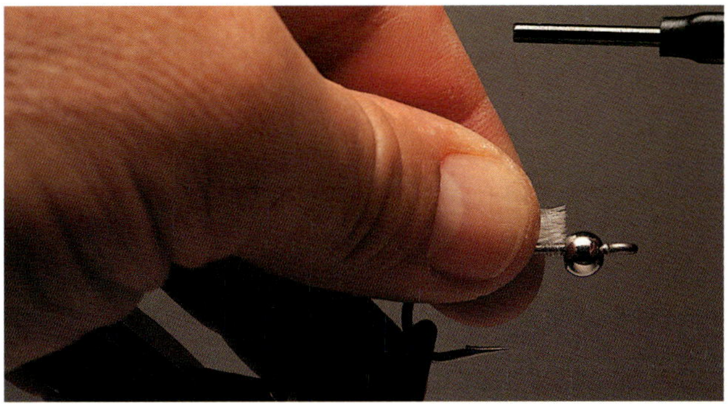

1. If desired or if necessary to accommodate the bead, crush the barb flat and slide the bead around to the hook eye. Wrap thread tightly against the bead to help keep it in place. Attach a bunch of Super Hair around the shank. Be sure to cut your hair butt ends square.

2. Before fastening the hair down securely, spread it around the shank with your thumb and index finger. Tighten the thread first at the rear of the tie-down point and work up toward the bead head. This will prevent a gap from developing behind the bead. Complete the fly according to the instructions for the basic Surf Candy. Note how the bead fits smoothly into the pattern. (Actual size, $3^5/_8$ inches)

RABBIT CANDIES

Although the regular Surf Candies work extremely well with hair, some tiers—and some fish—prefer more wiggle and action. Few materials provide this quality like rabbit fur strips. The leather hide does not provide the principal action, but rather the hair fibers, which move with the very slightest movement or water turbulence. Rabbit Candies are excellent for calm water situations or when fishing very slowly. We also use the Rabbit Candies only on small flies, since the hide will retain water, making the soggy fly inordinately heavy and difficult to cast. Here are two versions we use to achieve the desired action, which employ monofilament in different ways to keep the flies from fouling. You can interchange the several techniques shown here, using the mono loop of version 2 in conjunction with the fly design of version 1, for example.

Rabbit Candy (Version 1)

This variation utilizes the rabbit strip essentially in place of the hair as in the previous styles.

Materials

Super Hair or UltraHair (you can also use Craft Fur, Kinky Fiber, another synthetic, or bucktail)
Standard or short shank saltwater hook, commonly #2 through 1/0; Tiemco 800S used here
Fine monofilament thread
Flashabou, Krystal Flash, or other preferred flash
Devcon clear five-minute epoxy
Self-sticking prism eyes
Rabbit Zonker strip
Short piece of stiff mono, 20 to 30 pound-test
Pearl Flashabou in place of Super Hair or UltraHair

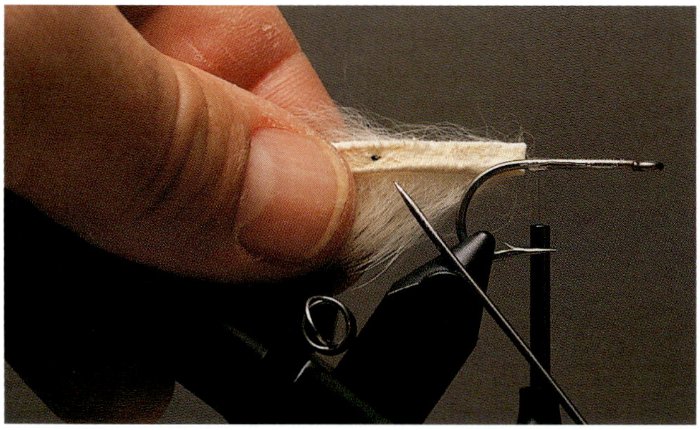

1. After attaching the thread to the hook shank, sear a hole with a dubbing needle, about 1/2 inch from the end of a strip of Zonker cut rabbit.

2. Using a lighter or match, melt the end of a stiff piece of 20- to 30-pound-test mono into a small ball shape. We do this *after* inserting the mono through the skin, since it is simpler to go through the hide side than the fur side.

3. Slide the rabbit up the mono until the melted ball is hidden inside the hair.

4. Fasten the mono to the hook shank with your thread. For durability, you can fold the mono through the eye and back along the shank so it is wrapped to the hook shank top and bottom.

5. Secure the end of the rabbit skin to the shank so it lies straight and trails to the rear.

6. In this sample, we used Sparkle Flash to give the fly added glow in the water, although you can use any of the regular hairs. All serve the same purpose of giving shape to the body by providing a form to hold the epoxy. Leave the flash or hair long enough to hold it with your materials hand while you are applying the epoxy.

7. The first coat of epoxy has been applied, as per the simple Surf Candy. Avoid getting epoxy on the rabbit fur. Wetting the fur slightly before using the epoxy will help keep it out of the way and under control.

8. A finished Rabbit Candy with eyes added and second coat of epoxy applied. (Fly shown actual size.)

Rabbit Candy (Version 2)

This variation uses the rabbit strip Zonker style.

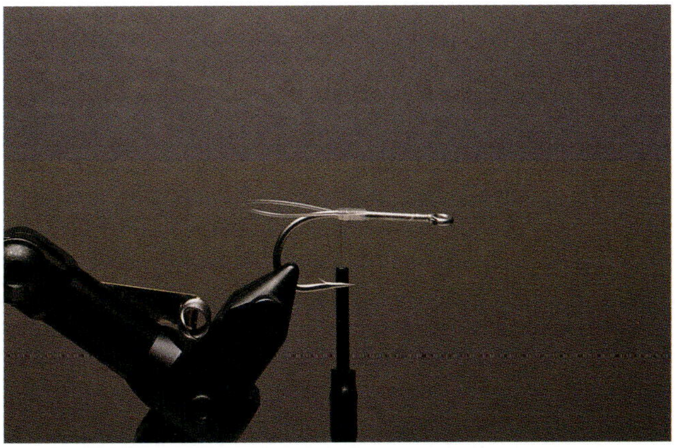

1. Tie a loop of heavy mono at the bend of the hook, fastening it securely on each side of the shank.

2. Moisten the rabbit fur, separate it, and tie it down at the bend.

3. Bring the thread forward and tie down the rabbit strip at the head. Tie in Super Hair underneath and on the sides of the shank.

4. The first epoxy coat is applied only to the hair on the bottom of the fly. The belly is painted silver and eyes are applied.

5. The final coat of epoxy is applied and the hair is trimmed, tapering toward the rear. (Actual size, 4 1/2 inches)

Wiggle Candy

Synthetics have come of age in the world of fly tying. One June a few years ago, a group of outdoor celebrities gathered at Montauk, New York. The weather was downright unpleasant, and the fish were uncooperative. While most of us picked a few fish, Lefty Kreh and his partner of the day stole the show with about three dozen bass, which he claimed "raced 10 feet to grab those wiggle tail flies." Preformed plastic wiggle tails can be added to the Surf Candy, like the Flexi Tail used here or the tail sections cut from a plastic lure known as a Redgill (see page 92) or the Fin-S Fish. Underwater videos show a terrifically lifelike wiggle using the Flexi Tails and Redgill tail sections. They seem to be a natural and logical addition to the Surf Candy. Some fly tiers feel that using formed plastic components violates something in their personal tying ethics. If that includes you, ignore these variations. We admit that these are examples of our experimentation and feel they may lead to other developments.

Materials

Super Hair or UltraHair (you can also use Craft Fur, Kinky Fiber, another synthetic, or bucktail)
Standard or short shank saltwater hook, commonly #2 through 1/0; Tiemco 800S used here
Fine monofilament thread
Flashabou, Krystal Flash, or other preferred flash
Devcon clear five-minute epoxy
Self-sticking prism eyes
Flexi Tail (from Rocky Mountain Dubbing)
Short piece of stiff mono, 20 to 30 pound-test
Cyanoacrylate (Krazy Glue or other)

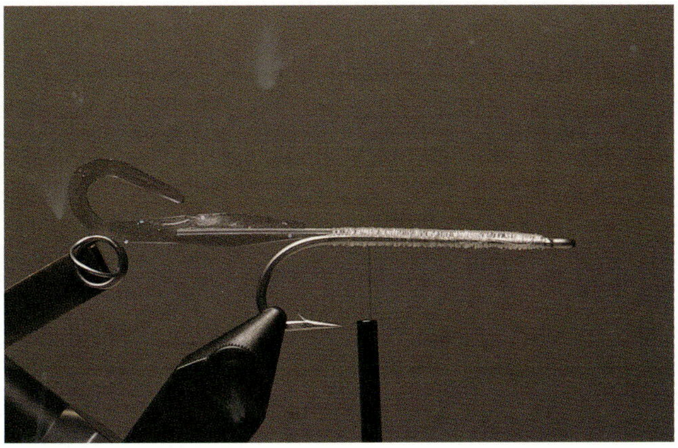

1. Attach a Flexi Tail to a section of stiff monofilament, using cyanoacrylate, such as Krazy Glue, and attach the tail extension to the hook.

2. The completed Wiggle Candy, with a Stick Candy body built around the shank, as above. (Fly shown actual size.)

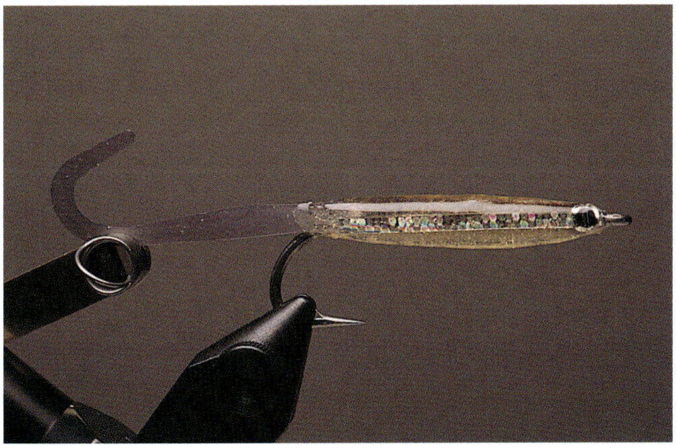

Version 2: A Wiggle Candy with the tail optionally attached directly to the hook shank. It's quicker, and a similar effect results, but in case of damage to the tail, it cannot be easily replaced, which is one of the advantages of using the mono extension technique. (Actual size, 2 1/4 inches)

Bonito Candy

This variation was so named after we had exceptional success while fishing for bonito in Connecticut and Rhode Island. Several small, thin saddle hackle points with no webbing are tied near the bend. Then the hair is added and the fly completed like the simple Surf Candy. This gives a seductive little wiggle to the lure. We tied this sample with bucktail. (Actual size, 3 1/2 inches)

Stick Candy

This is simply a Surf Candy adapted to a long-shank hook and tied very thin to replicate a sand eel or other skinny bait. Note, too, that the eyes are placed well forward. An elver imitation called the Candy Eel (not shown) is a slight variation, using a regular-length hook, longer hair, and eye placement farther to the rear. (Actual size, 3 1/2 inches)

Sea Candy

To simulate very large sand eels, anchovies, mackerel, and the like, we use a large, strong hook and upsize the whole fly. The imitation here (actual size, 6 1/2 inches), shown alongside a small Surf Candy spearing, was tied to imitate a baby bluefish, a popular forage for many game species. Note that the hook is positioned in the lower third of the body to afford good hook gape. This feature, plus the flattened sides of the head, cannot be achieved with a drying wheel. It must be made by hand manipulation. There is no substitute for thorough knowledge of epoxy modeling. Although it is sometimes possible to use a single coat of epoxy on certain smaller flies, due to the large amount of epoxy required here, two coats are a must, as with the 'Cuda Candy following. See also the chapter on "Additional Pop Fleyes" for other large fly techniques.

'Cuda Candy

Barracuda flies are typically very long, in imitation of the fish's favorite prey, the needlefish. In this case also, a drying wheel was not used, not only for the reasons just stated for the Sea Candy, but also because of the inordinate length of the hair. (Actual size, 7 3/4 inches)

Keel Eel

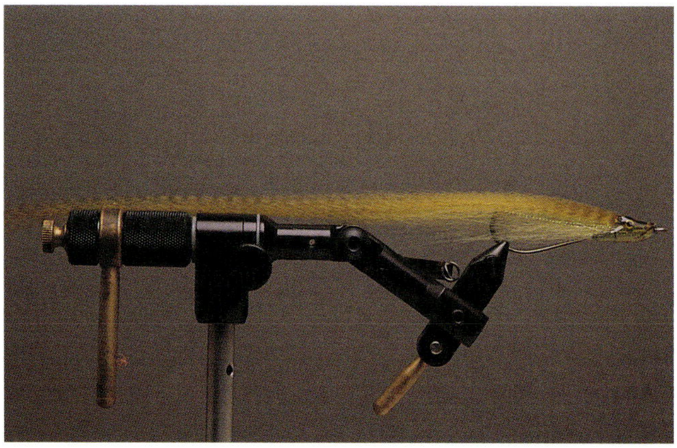

Working sandy, weedy, and rocky bottoms can cause lots of hangups. If you flirt with obstructions of any type, a bendback hook will solve the problem. We use imitations like the one shown here to imitate American eels. As with the 'Cuda Candy and Sea Candy, this one calls for a little added manipulation to keep the epoxy from sagging under the hook. The eye is small and placed high. The epoxy is extended farther underneath, and a mouth is added with a marker between the two coats of epoxy. The epoxy on top must be kept short to avoid closing the hook gap. (Actual size, 10 3/4 inches)

JIGGIES

We probably tie and use more of these simple creations currently than any other fly discussed in this book. In the tradition of the Clouser Deep Minnow, this fly yields a streamlined silhouette and enticingly drops between strips. One advantage is that the cone heads can't break off. Also, the Jiggy is not an epoxy fly in the same sense as the flies described above. Epoxy, while an essential component, is only used to give flow to the design and provide the wrappings with durable protection. It is not used to form or shape the actual fly body. It is one of the few patterns for which we regularly use and advise a drying wheel, which facilitates forming nice, rounded heads. We generally use bucktail for its natural taper and opaque characteristics, although false albacore and bonito in particular seem to respond to Jiggies of Super Hair or UltraHair.

We show here two slight variations on the Jiggy (and there are others), one with a bendback design, the other without. The bendback hook partially conceals the hook point and gives the fly a slightly different line; it has nothing to do with the attitude of the sinking fly, nor does lead on the shank or lead eyes or cones.

Since Jiggies require only one coat of epoxy, applied as the final step, we usually make up a large number of flies and then do all the epoxy work at one time, using thirty-minute epoxy and the rotating drying wheel.

False albacore caught on a Jiggy at Harkers Island, North Carolina.

A bead-head Jiggy took this bass from a New Jersey flat in early spring.

Weakfish of 5 1/2 pounds, caught on a Jiggy at Barnegat Bay, New Jersey.

A roosterfish taken from the Baja surf on a Jiggy.

Jiggy (bucktail version)

Materials

Silver, gold, or black cone or Jiggy head

Tiemco 911S or other long-shank hook, bendback optional

Fine monofilament thread

Bucktail

Flashabou or Krystal Flash

Devcon clear five-minute epoxy

Self-sticking prism eyes

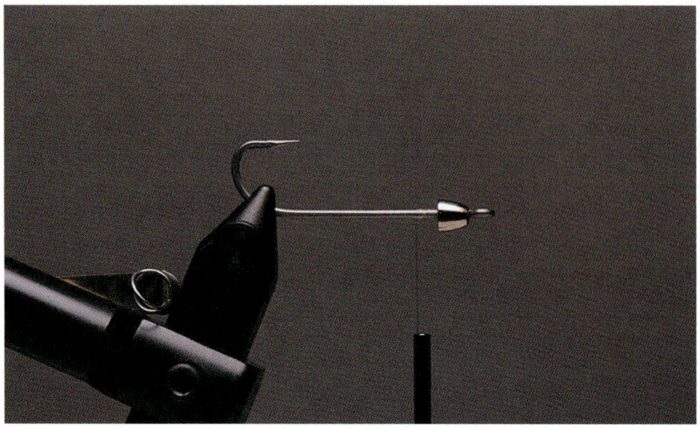

1. Bend the barb flat if desired or necessary to accommodate the cone. Slide the cone to the hook eye and attach the tying thread close behind it.

2. Attach sparse bucktail, roughly twice the length of the hook shank, close behind the cone. It is important that the hair be tied *only on the top* of the hook shank.

3. Add desired flash on top of the bucktail. Here we have used Krystal Flash.

4. Add more bucktail of a similar or contrasting color on top of the flash.

5. Add a prism eye on each side of the fly over the wraps, and hold them in place with two wraps of the clear thread. This will ensure that the eyes stay put and the thread will virtually disappear when the epoxy is added.

6. Whip-finish and tie off the thread close behind the cone.

7. Cover only the eyes and wraps with epoxy. Only one coat is required.

8. Rotate the vise as needed. Note the bare hook shank and absence of hair on the underside.

9. Finished bucktail Jiggy, shown actual size.

Jiggy (Super Hair version)

Materials

Silver, gold, or black cone or Jiggy head
Tiemco 911S or other long-shank hook, bendback optional
Fine monofilament thread
Super Hair
Flashabou or Krystal Flash
Devcon clear five-minute epoxy
Self-sticking prism eyes

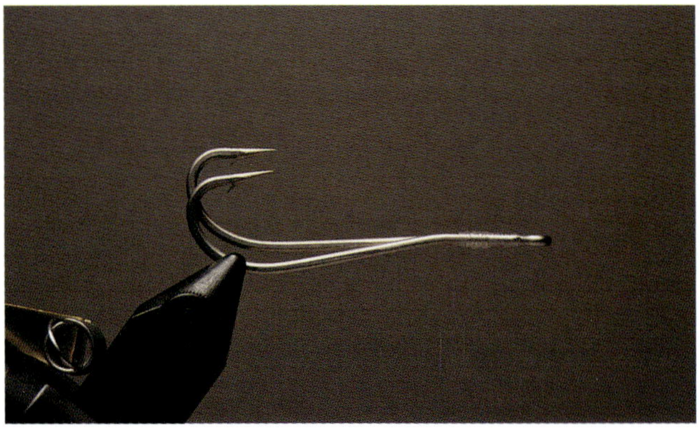

1. Although you can tie the fly without bending the shank, you can sometimes give the fly better flow and appearance with a bendback. Here is the precise amount of bend we recommend if you want to use the bendback technique. More bend than this may cause you to miss strikes. Note that you will get a softer bend if you bend the shank by hand, or hold the hook loosely with pliers and bend by pushing down on the bend of the hook with your finger, which is not very difficult with the longer-shank hook we use. Doing most of the bending by twisting it with pliers gives a sharper bend and may weaken some hooks significantly.

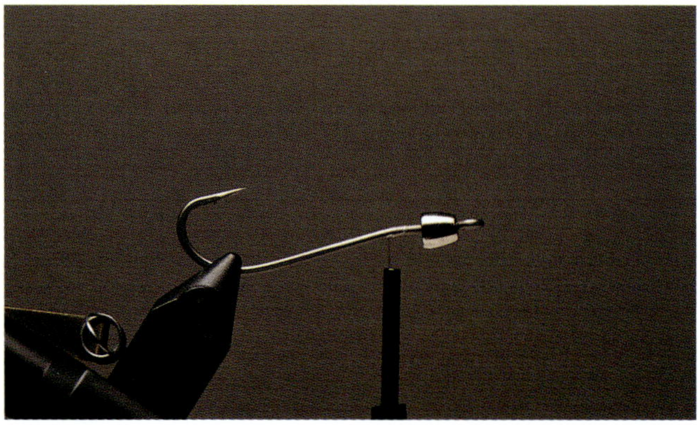

2. Bend the barb down if necessary or desired, and slide the cone around to the eye. Attach thread behind the cone.

3. Flash is added on top of shank. (Angel Hair is used here.) In this case, the flash provides side reflectance as from scales and the medial stripe.

4. A second, shorter bunch is added underneath to simulate the shiny belly sac of many baits. Note that although we advocate tying all the wing hair on the top side, to keep the fly riding properly, the small amount of nonbuoyant material underneath the shank will have little effect on upsetting the balance of the fly.

5. Super Hair is tied on top of the shank, in this case tan to simulate the back color of a bay anchovy.

6. Prism eyes are added and secured with two wraps of the monofilament tying thread.

7. Applying epoxy.

8. You can turn the fly by hand, in your rotating vise, or on an electric drying wheel until the epoxy sets.

9. The finished Jiggy, shown actual size. One even coat of epoxy is all that is generally required.

Bob Popovics worked with manufacturer Stu Dickens, of Bestco Enterprises, to develop a special cone head for another modified version of his Jiggy. This slightly heavier lead head produces better jigging action, has flat surfaces on the sides to receive prism eyes so that they are farther forward, and is notched on either side to snug up against the hook eye and prevent turning. It also features a larger hole, so it is easier to slide around the hook bend and makes it unnecessary to flatten the barb on most hooks, an advantage for those who want to fish barbed hooks.

You can also wrap several turns of lead or other wire around the shank and push it inside the cone. This slight addition of lead is used more to produce better fly action than it is to sink the fly. As an option, you can also wrap some fine chenille around the shank and force it into the cavity of the head from the rear to secure it more firmly against the hook eye.

A finished doubleheader Jiggy. (Actual size, 4 7/8 inches)

A Jiggy tied with a Jiggy head, specifically designed for this fly.

A Jiggy tied with a rabbit fur strip and a bead head used in place of a cone.

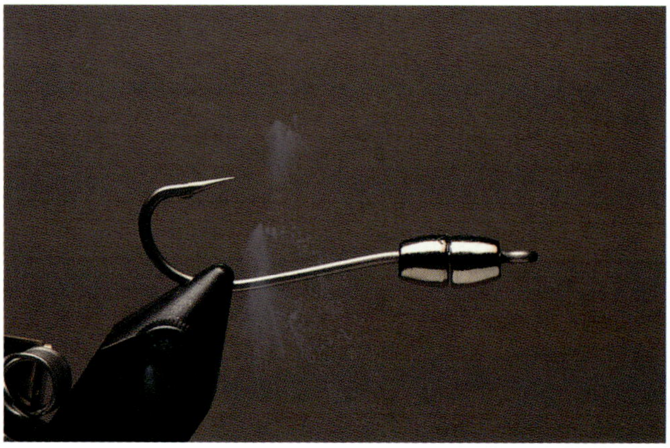

Two cones can be used for extra weight and more jigging action.

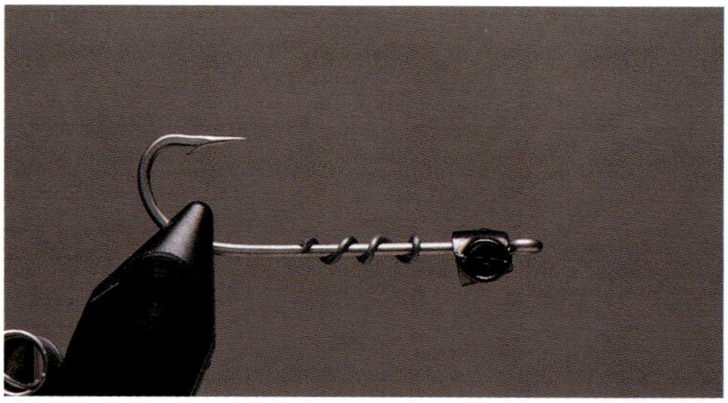

To increase the weight of a Jiggy head, wrap several turns of lead wire around the hook shank . . .

. . . and push the wire inside the head.

Fishing Tip: Loop Knot

You will get the best results when fishing Jiggies if you connect them to your leader tippet with a loop knot. Your flies will swing, dance, and jig more freely. We prefer the nonslip mono loop knot.

Also, when a mono shock tippet is required for other flies—for example, when fishing around rock jetties, when using large flies for large striped bass, or when pursuing snook, tarpon, or other rough-mouthed fish that can abrade your leader—the loop knot will minimize the heavy leader's interference with fly action. It isn't difficult to tie and is very reliable.

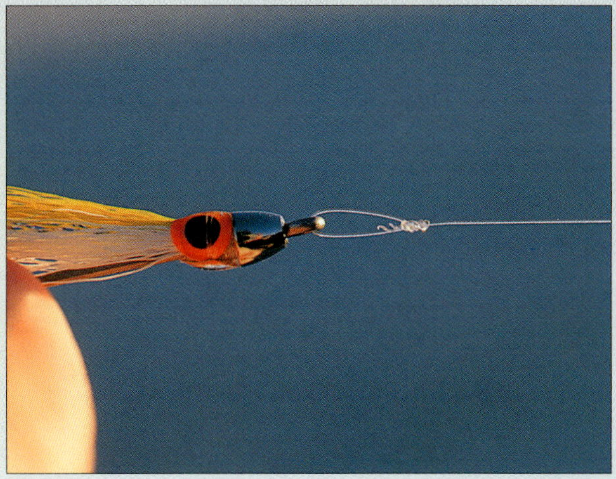

The Jiggy works best when tied into a loop knot.

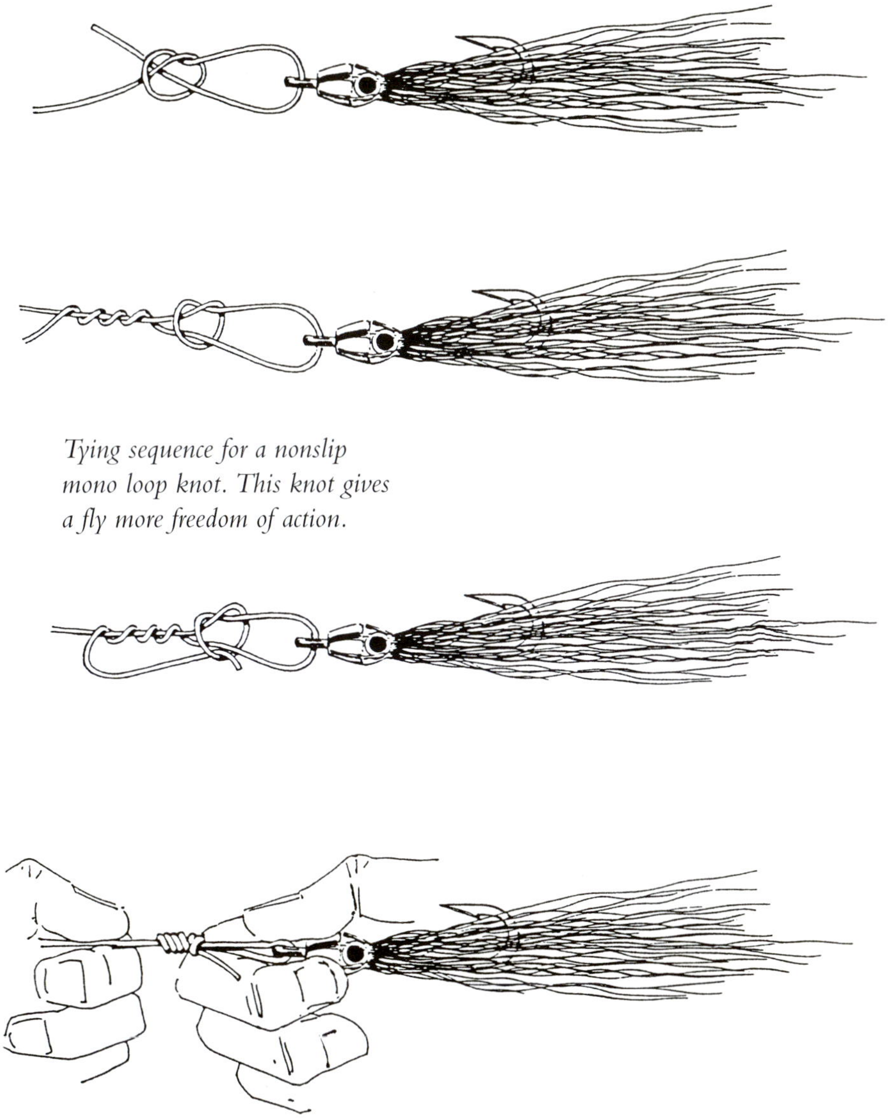

Tying sequence for a nonslip mono loop knot. This knot gives a fly more freedom of action.

Fishing Tip: Retrieving Weighted Flies

Getting the fly to the proper depth in the water column is all important in most fishing situations. To get deeper, use a sinking line. After you cast, count down a few seconds, then start your retrieve. After several attempts without success, count a bit longer. It helps to use less-buoyant materials if you want to get your flies deeper, too. The principle idea behind adding weight to the front end of a fly, like the Deep Candy, Jiggy, or Clouser Minnow is to adjust the attitude and action of the fly. Count on your weighted line not the front weight on the fly, to carry it into the depths. When you retrieve a front-loaded fly, strip and pause, allowing the fly to drop between the strips so that the tinsel and hair wiggle enticingly. Some anglers claim front-loaded flies are merely jigs. In reality, you can't jig a fly, which is tethered to a fly line, in the same manner as a lead-headed jig worked on a spinning rod with monofilament line.

When fishing a weighted fly, don't always retrieve it immediately. Count down while it sinks.

Use intermittent strips of the line to make the fly swim in an erratic, up-and-down fashion. This effectively simulates a wounded or disoriented baitfish.

Schoolie

This unique creation evolved when we were deciding how to simulate small baits that were disproportionate to the larger hooks needed to hook and hold striped bass. We observed that although bass seized one large mullet or herring at a time, they tended to take smaller baits by the mouthful, as many as a dozen or more, depending on the size. We imitated these "meatballs" of bait by fashioning two, three, or four flies on one large keel hook. When retrieved, the small school moves in unison, precisely like the naturals the fish are accustomed to seeing.

Materials

Super Hair or UltraHair (you can also use Craft Fur, Kinky Fiber, another synthetic, or bucktail
Keel hook
Fine monofilament thread
Flashabou, Krystal Flash, or other preferred flash
Devcon clear five-minute Epoxy
Self-sticking prism eyes
Red Sharpie permanent marker, fine or medium point

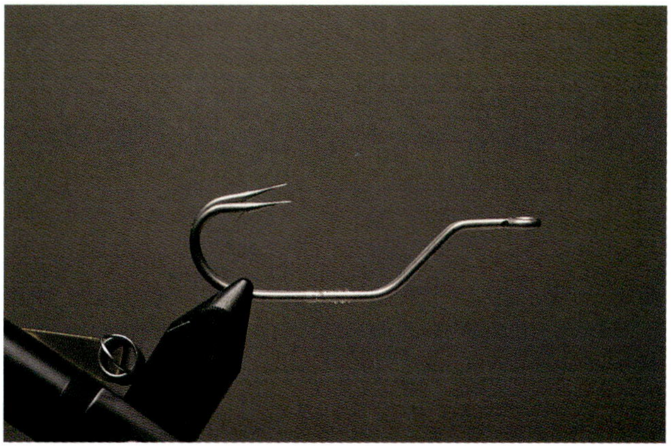

1. Open the hook gap slightly before you begin to tie.

2. Size up the length of the two flies by gauging against the top shank.

3. Tie a small fly on the front portion of the lower hook shank. This one is tied with UltraHair and a bit of flash.

4. Tie a second fly around the short upper shank, just behind the eye. Give the heads one coat of epoxy and trim the hair. (Fly shown actual size.)

Optional: If you want to add a third fly, construct it first, on a piece of monofilament (see "Tying with Two Vises," page 114). Tie in the bottom fly, then attach the end of the mono to the diagonal section of the shank and tie the topmost fly. We have made Schoolies with as many as five flies attached to one hook.

Spread Fly (butterfish)

Wide, flat-profile baitfish like herring or butterfish can present a challenge for tiers. The Spread Fly exploits silhouette. It gives an impression of more size and mass than it possesses. This is a two-dimensional fly, using epoxy to maintain its shape and form, but it is very light and eminently castable, and you can make it as thin as an envelope if desired. Unlike the Surf Candy, the body of which is essentially constructed of epoxy, the Spread Fly uses little epoxy, but directed to a very specific function. In that, it follows a line of thinking similar to that for the Jiggy and Schoolie. The Spread Fly is very tier friendly, an easy route to rewarding results. Because it is so sparse and lacks buoyancy, it is also a fly suited to the use of synthetic hair. We tie it almost exclusively with Super Hair or UltraHair. The sample shown here imitates a butterfish profile, to emphasize the possibilities of the technique, but the spread needn't be so extreme for other baitfish imitations.

Materials

Regular-length stainless hook
Fine monofilament thread
Super Hair or UltraHair
Devcon clear five-minute epoxy
Kodak Photo-Flo solution (available in camera shops)
Self-sticking prism eyes

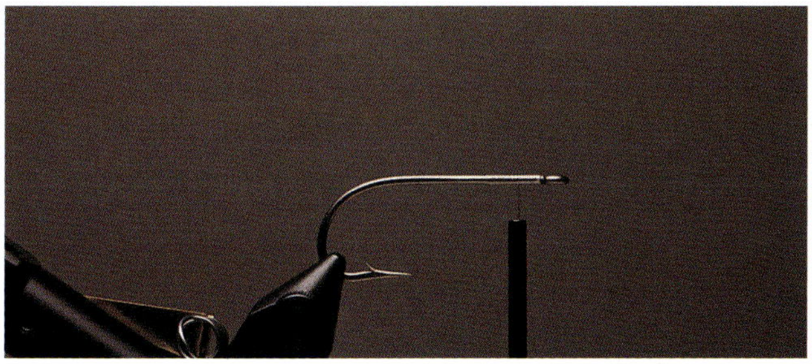

1. Attach the thread close to the eye and don't bring it back farther than shown.

2. Attach a bunch of hair behind the eye and distribute it around the hook shank evenly. We used two-tone UltraHair here, but you can use a solid color or blend shades together. (See the discussion on synthetic hairs, page 20, for how to do this.)

3. Put some flash sparsely around the shank over the hair and tie off the thread. The tying is now complete.

4. Put clear five-minute epoxy over the front portion of the hair, no more than one-quarter to one-third of the length of the hook shank.

5. Work epoxy into the hair with your bodkin.

6. When the epoxy has stopped flowing freely and is nearly set (after approximately four minutes), moisten your index finger and thumb with Photo-Flo solution and squeeze the epoxy firmly.

7. The hair will spread to the desired shape, depending on the amount of pressure you apply.

8. Press the eyes in place and apply a second coat of epoxy.

9. Trim the excess hair, and the fly is complete. (Shown actual size.)

Top view of the butterfish Spread Fly, showing the thin, flat cross section.

A more moderate Spread Fly imitates a herring.

A snapper bluefish Spread Fly.

A baby bunker Spread Fly.

Bob Popovics holds a large blue spread fly that fooled this dorado caught by Lance Erwin under floating grass in the Baja.

Capt. Brady Bounds with a Potomac River striper that fell for the same fly as the dorado pictured above.

Ultra Shrimp

The physical characteristics of shrimp, particularly their smooth, semihard bodies and translucence, lend themselves well to imitation with epoxy. Chumming with grass shrimp is a popular method for enticing striped bass, spotted sea trout, and weakfish into casting range. When fish are seen in the chum line, the fly fisherman substitutes the Ultra Shrimp, fished dead drift or with occasional twitches. Many spin fishermen also use the Popovics Ultra Shrimp (as well as the Jiggy) as a teaser or dropper fly ahead of a swimming plug.

Materials

Super Hair or UltraHair (you can also use Craft Fur, Kinky Fiber, another synthetic, or bucktail)
Standard or short shank saltwater hook, commonly #2 through 1/0; Tiemco 800S used here
Fine monofilament thread
Flashabou, Krystal Flash, or other preferred flash
Devcon clear five-minute epoxy
Self-sticking prism eyes
Short pieces of stiff mono, 20 to 30 pound-test
Saddle hackle, color to complement body

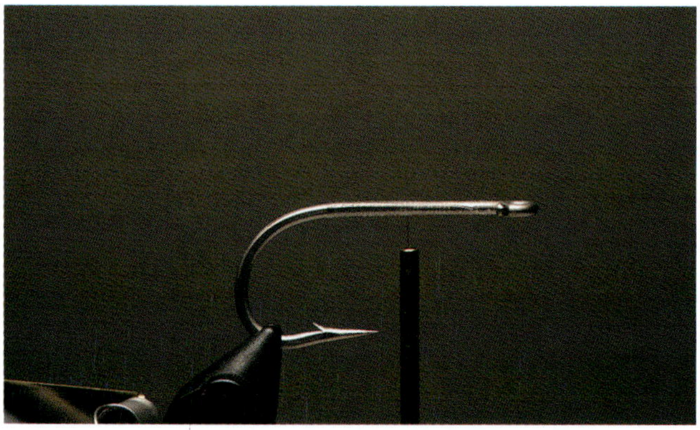

1. Attach the thread to the shank and leave it about midshank.

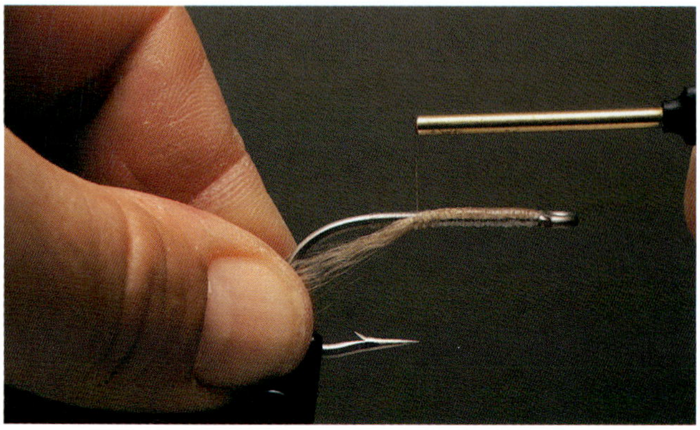

2. Tie in a sparse bunch of tan UltraHair along the top of the hook shank, wrapping thread up to the hook eye and back to midshank. Pull the hair downward and . . .

3. . . . continue wrapping so that the hair is cocked downward. This simulates the walking legs.

4. Tie a smaller, shorter bunch of UltraHair atop this and extending to the rear, to simulate the mouthparts.

5. Melt the ends of two pieces of stiff 20-pound-test mono into small balls for the eyes, as shown for the Rabbit Candy (page 42). You can color these with permanent felt marking pens if desired. Or, since some shrimp have bright luminous eyes (see photo on page 18), you can paint them with a spot of phosphorescent paint. Tie one eye stem on each side of the shank so that they protrude slightly to the rear of the bend. With your thread, build up the underbody of the fly.

6. Fasten a tan saddle hackle, butt first, to the shank near the bend.

7. Lay a few strands of Flashabou or Krystal Flash along the top of the hook and secure them with the thread.

8. Wrap the hackle, palmer style, toward the eye. Make the first few wraps close together, then space them out a little as you approach the eye.

9. Trim the hackle across the top, leaving fibers underneath to simulate the swimming legs and on the sides to stabilize the fly in the water. Trim away any excess material over the eye and move the thread to just behind the eye.

10. Tie a long bunch of hair along the top of the shank to simulate the carapace. Fasten with thread only behind the eye, allowing some to extend forward over the eye, to represent the tail or telson.

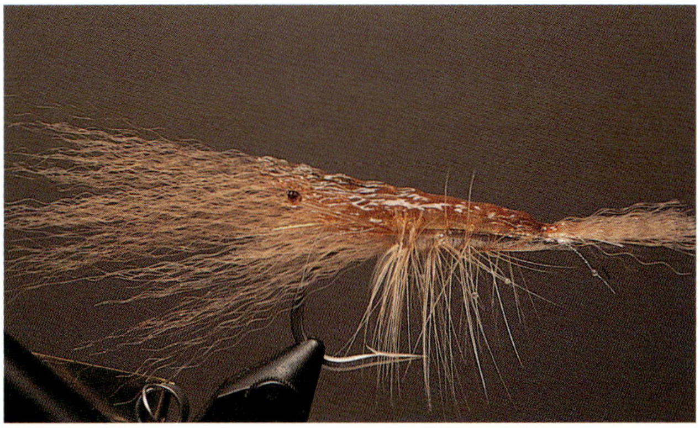

11. Apply the first coat of epoxy along the top of the fly, from the wraps behind the hook eye to just slightly beyond the bend. Going too far with the epoxy could impede hooking. Also, do not put epoxy on the shrimp tail, the hairs protruding over the hook eye. This may make the fly retrieve off line and makes threading with the leader more difficult.

12. Trim the tail of the shrimp straight across and the head at an angle as shown. Optionally, you can leave a few very long fibers extending to the rear to simulate the antennae. We opted to cut them off in this sample, since they would not be included in the photograph frame anyway.

13. Apply the second coat of epoxy to produce a smooth finish. You may eliminate it if you prefer the rougher finish and lighter weight of one coat. Note that we have intentionally left some droplets on the hackle fibers, as sometimes happens. If this occurs when tying the fly, *do not attempt to wipe them off.* Wait until the epoxy is completely dry and hard.

14. The finished fly, shown actual size. Notice that the beads of epoxy have been pulled off the hackle with no adverse effect.

15. The finished Ultra Shrimp, top view.

16. The finished Ultra Shrimp, head-on view.

Fishing Tip: Fishing the Ultra Shrimp

The Ultra Shrimp is the most realistic and successful grass shrimp imitation in use along the east coast. You can fish it, dead drift, around shoreline grass beds or under floating mats of eel grass. You can also fish it in a current at a predetermined depth by attaching a strike indicator to your leader and along the fly to drift along with the tide. This is a favorite procedure of New Jersey striper anglers fishing canals and creeks. A superproductive technique is to chum the water with grass shrimp. These can be netted from bay waters or purchased from bait shops by the quart. Throw only a few at a time, every minute or so, into the current, allowing them to drift with the tide, usually near inlets or along jetties. After ten minutes, let your fly drift back into the slick with the line just taut enough to detect a pickup, but not enough to inhibit the drift of the fly. Weakfish and stripers have succumbed to this technique for generations.

Candy Squid

Baby squid school in enormous numbers and are a prominent food source of many ocean game fish. Here's how to make a realistic imitation employing the epoxy methods used for the other patterns included in this chapter. We chose tan/brown for this sample for no particular reason other than that it is a fairly common neutral color (see the photo on page 18). Squids occur in a variety of colors, depending on the species, their aggressive or relaxed posture, and whether they are fed or empty, evacuated or filled with ink. Also see chapters four and five for more squid patterns.

Materials

Super Hair or UltraHair (you can also use Craft Fur, Kinky Fiber, another synthetic, or bucktail)
Standard or short shank saltwater hook, commonly # 2 through 1/0; Tiemco 800S used here
Fine monofilament thread
Flashabou, Krystal Flash, or other preferred flash
Devcon clear five-minute epoxy
Self-sticking prism eyes
Red Sharpie permanent marker, fine or medium point
Rubber Sililegs
Black marking pen
Gold braid piping

1. Tie a short clump of Super Hair around the shank at the bend. This will support and separate the tentacles.

2. Add a small amount of Krystal Flash around the hair.

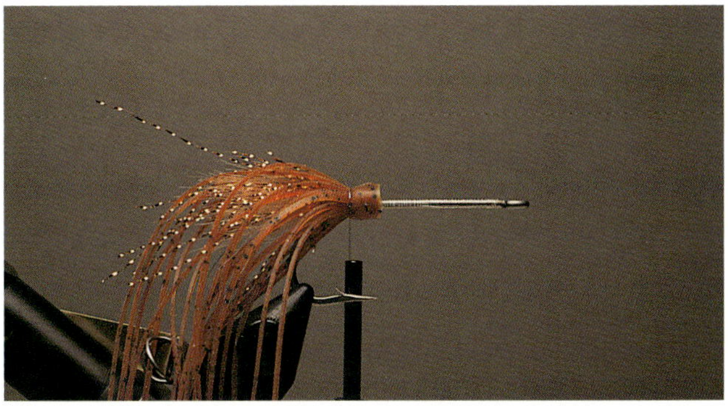

3. Attach a section of Sililegs rubber skirt material such as used for spinner baits. Wrap it around the shank and tie down securely.

4. Attach Body Braid or piping at the bend of the hook.

5. Wrap braided piping around the shank, building up the underbody with a taper toward the hook eye.

6. Attach Super Hair, spread all around the shank, and tie off the thread. Make the fibers long so that you can handle them easily. Their purpose is to form an understructure for the epoxy; much of the excess length will be trimmed away.

7. Apply the first coat of epoxy, working it between the fibers as for the regular Surf Candy, from the eye to the bend of the hook.

8. Place a dominant eye on each side, near the start of the bend of the hook.

9. Apply the second coat of epoxy over the body and add spots with a permanent marking pen.

10. Trim away all the excess hair extending beyond the epoxy, leaving just a feathered edge protruding from the epoxy.

11. Trim the legs to a length proportionate to the overall fly. Hold a few out of the way and leave them long to simulate the long tentacles of the squid.

12. The finished Candy Squid, shown actual size.

Fishing Tip: Varying Retrieves

Different flies call for different retrieves. Mullet, squid, and shrimp, for example, all act differently in the water. Learn how each behaves and maneuvers, and try to copy their motions with your fly. You can retrieve a fly steadily, with no pause in motion at any rate from superslow to superfast. You can also impart pulsating, stop-and-start movements to your fly. Or you can make long, sweeping strips. Experiment with the frequency, speed, and length of your line strips.

Bob Popovics using a two-handed retrieve.

Capt. Brady Bounds works a fly with a long, one-handed strip.

Chapter Four

Silicone Pop Fleyes

WORKING WITH SILICONE

Silicone is another synthetic, nontraditional fly-tying substance that has further opened the door to wonderful fly-tying creativity. Silicone is a synthetic rubber compound, and its unique qualities make it admirably suited to certain fly-tying operations. It holds its shape and has a spongy texture, flexibility, buoyancy, durability, and a much greater working time than epoxy. After testing other colors, we have settled upon clear, which is actually slightly milky and semitranslucent, for our tying operations. You may find black or white useful for your purposes. You can purchase silicone in tubes and squeeze it out as needed, like toothpaste. If you find you enjoy working with silicone, buy a larger cylinder and use it in a caulking gun, precisely the same setup you use for applying bathtub and tile sealer.

We have used a half dozen different commercial brands and found they all work satisfactorily, although some are a bit clearer or softer than others. It's largely a matter of personal choice. One of us prefers DAP, made by Dow Chemicals; the other likes GE Silicone II Household Glue and Seal. Silicone is inexpensive, so try a few different makes and decide for yourself.

You will also require a wetting agent to use with the silicone; otherwise it sticks to your finger almost like chewing gum when you remove it from the fly. We experimented with several substances and found Kodak Photo-Flo Solution, available at camera shops, to be excellent. A small bottle will last most tiers for years. In the instructions below, we'll describe how and when to use it.

You can use liquid dishwashing detergent, but if you go that route, get clear detergent, since colored liquids

LEFTY KREH

will tint your finished flies. Glycerin, available at drugstores, also works, but not quite so effectively or neatly.

As when working with epoxy, you can work off disposable self-stick note papers or squeeze silicone directly onto your finger or the fly, which is generally what we do. Keep some facial tissues or paper towels on hand for quick cleanup and to wipe the material from your fingers. Use the tissues also to blot excess wetting agent from the fly. In addition to your fingertip, a disposable plastic knife blade is a useful tool to smear the material onto the fly, especially when reaching underneath into the hook gape. If the knife has a serrated edge, file or grind it smooth to avoid striations in the silicone. In between uses, keep your silicone capped, or hard lumps will form at the mouth of the tube. Also, keep the top of your table clear and clean when using either epoxy or silicone. Stray bits of marabou fluff, tinsel, and hair have a way of getting into these materials.

As we suggested with epoxy, experiment with this material, and you'll soon learn how to handle it effectively for many tying uses. It doesn't have the relatively short working time of epoxy, and there is no fear of running or sagging, so you can work at a more leisurely pace while sculpting your flies. Allow some curing time, however. Although you can fish with them soon after completion, we prefer to let silicone flies sit overnight for full curing.

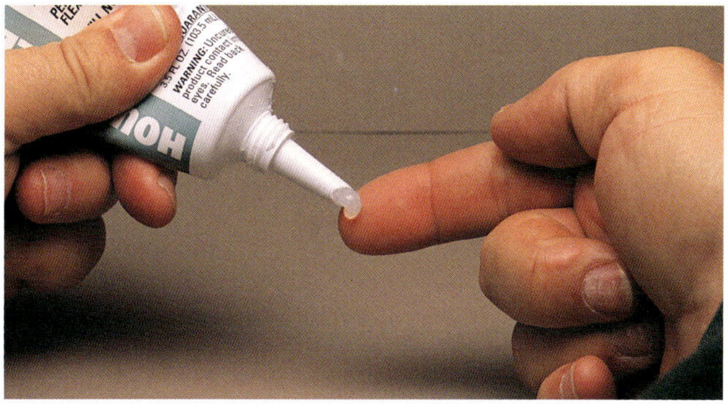

Use your fingertip to apply silicone.

Wet your finger with Photo-Flo or another wetting agent when smoothing out silicone.

SILICLONES

The genesis of the Siliclone again represents the Pop Fleyes approach to fly design: creativity with a purpose. Its history is much like that of the epoxy Surf Candy. The combination of the two principal materials, sheep fleece and silicone, each employed for a specific purpose, evolved from two separate incidents.

Bob had tied a small crab imitation, fashioning the body from clipped deer hair, as others had done. He then coated it with silicone to give it the feel of a softshell crab, a favorite striped bass food. Visually the fly was fine, and many tiers would have been thrilled with the results. But it tended to float instead of sink, which required inordinate weighting to overcome the natural buoyancy of both materials, and generally it didn't behave the way Bob wanted. For the time, he gave up on the pattern.

At a later date, he fashioned a streamer fly with a wool head, such as is commonly used for a Muddler Minnow variation. Bluefish liked the fly but promptly tore the fleece apart. Eventually, after recalling the earlier crab experiment and experimenting with different materials to achieve the desired texture and behavior, coupled with requisite durability, the first Siliclones were born. The experimentation in the meanwhile was as intense as it was time-consuming.

Trimmed deer hair had limited durability. It couldn't retain its shape when subjected to the rigors of the salt environment and saltwater fish, although the Muddler Minnow design was a good starting point. Also, spinning and trimming hair is a time-consuming chore. The Wool Head Muddler and flies like Bob Johns' Widow Maker were closer to what we wanted. But they soaked up water, sank, became harder to cast in large sizes, and didn't perform the way we wanted. We desired a fly that had near neutral density, could be made to wake when fished slowly, and even float at rest, behaving like the crankbaits and swimming plugs we had used on spinning tackle. Also, many saltwater fish, not just bluefish, are rough on flies. Striped bass will tear up tinsel and ruin deer hair in short order, distorting and misshaping them. Durability, then, was a key requirement.

We first took advantage of the myriad possibilities of clipped sheep fleece, or ram's wool, coated with silicone, by imitating one of the commonest baits that sweep past mid-Atlantic beaches in hordes during the fall, the white or finger mullet. These mullet, typically 4 to 6 inches in length, generally have rounded heads, actually somewhat flattened on top to give a slightly triangular form, and thick bodies, which are opaque. In swimming, they often make a slight bulge or wake of "nervous water." Buoyancy was a feature to appreciate. Our fascination with silicone and the popularity of scientific cloning in the 1990s combined to produce the name. Siliclone flies can be made to swim at or near the surface, due to the natural buoyancy of the materials employed in combination, bucktail and silicone-coated fleece, coupled with the construction method, which traps air in the head. We learned that all the characteristics of the mullet—shape, silhouette, size, opacity, and behavior—could be admirably copied with the Siliclone. When pulled, the fly would dive slightly and pop back to the surface when we paused on the retrieve. If the fly eventually absorbed water and began to sink slowly, we could continue to fish it as an underwater lure or simply take the fly from the water and squeeze the head to force out the water and restore the buoyancy. If we wanted it to sink, we could hold it underwater and squeeze the head. This allowed the head to fill with water and develop a slow-sinking, near-neutral buoyancy.

We realized, too, that bulk contributed another important dimension to this fly design. The water resistance against the head of the fly, like a small boxing glove pushing water, created vibrations in the water and minor currents of turbulence, which made the bucktail move enticingly. When cast, it made a distinctive surface splat that attracted fish, particularly around rockpiles and other structure. Perhaps this mimics the smacking surface blips that bunker make. Various shapes could also be modeled: round, oval, tapered, fat, or thin. A family of flies, similar to but smaller than that generated by the epoxy Surf Candy, evolved.

From experience and familiarity with the substance, we learned to employ silicone selectively, to shape and protect other patterns not involving fleece, like the 3D and Cotton Candy designs. Artificials with oval, round, or triangular cross sections and cylindrical cigar shapes were a real possibility. Most traditional streamer fly designs tend to be vertical in cross section, since hackles are typically arranged in such a way that they give a more-or-less flat profile when viewed from the front, much like hands placed with palms together.

As with all our flies, we tested the Siliclones in a broad range of waters and situations, fresh and salt, as we developed them. Lefty Kreh tested them on the New River in West Virginia, and his smallmouth guide was so excited about the flies' success that he said, "Lefty, you can leave the boat but those flies are staying." Bob Clouser handed an early version to a client on the Susquehanna River, with the disclaimer that the bugs weren't worked out yet. The client hooked the largest bass of the trip on his third cast and announced that it suited him just fine. The first few years we tested them in the surf, we took the majority of our large bass and blues on them. It remains our number-one probing fly for night fishing, especially in a calm surf and in slow rivers and tidal creeks. Ever since these flies made their debut at shows and fly shops, they have received widespread positive reaction and acceptance from tiers and fishermen. They have also long been produced commercially by Umpqua Feather Merchants. Like the other Pop Fleyes discussed in these pages, the Siliclone is not a specific pattern, calling for precise materials and colors applied in one way. It is a concept, a widely adaptable and applicable technique, evolved from a well-defined idea.

Siliclone (Mullet)

Materials

Heavy model perfect hook, Partridge Homosassa or similar style
Fine monofilament thread
Bucktail
Sheep fleece or ram's wool
Wire brush or comb
Clear silicone
Kodak Photo-Flo solution
Self-sticking prism eyes

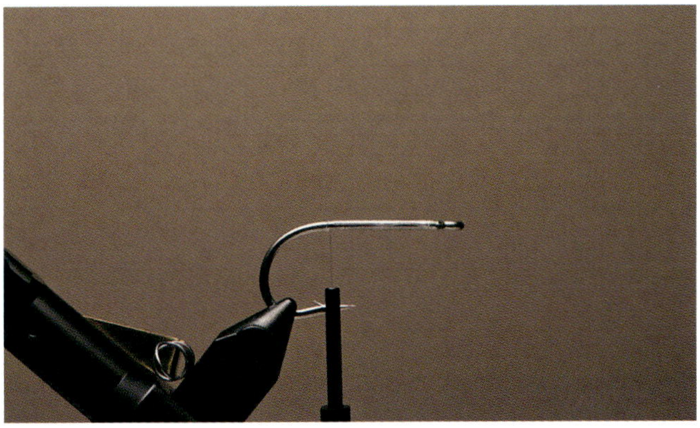

1. Start with the thread near the bend of the hook shank.

2. Tie in a bunch of bucktail about two times the hook length, distributing the hair evenly around the shank.

3. Add a smaller, shorter bunch of bucktail neatly distributed off to each side, to provide the "shoulders" to the fly. This helps the form as well as balance and buoyancy of the fly.

4. Top view showing the effect of adding the shoulders to widen the body.

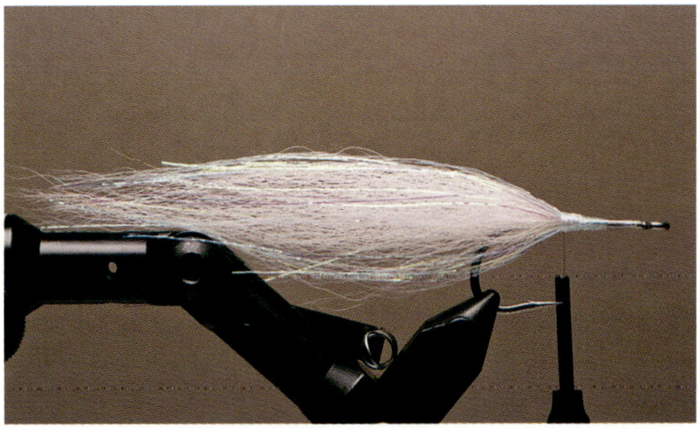

5. Add some flash around the bucktail (optional), trimming the ends to different length for better flash effect.

6. Brush the sheep fleece with a wire dog comb to get rid of tangles.

7. Cut a small tuft of fleece from the hide.

8. Push it back over the shank from the eye so the tips of the fleece face the rear, making certain that it is distributed evenly around the shank. Hold the fleece with your materials hand while you catch it with two loose wraps of thread.

9. Pull the thread taut to tie down the fleece securely. This forms a veil of material, covering the wraps around the base of the bucktail and blending the head and tail components smoothly, to give the fly an aesthetic flow.

10. Holding back the fleece with your materials hand, work the thread forward through the fleece so that it is in front of the first bunch of fleece.

11. Prepare a second tuft of fleece, but cut off the tips.

12. Push the fleece over the shank from the eye, so that it is evenly distributed around the shank.

13. Switch the fleece and hold it in place with the fingers of your materials hand . . .

14. . . . while you wrap two loose turns of thread around the fleece.

15. Cinch it down tightly with a few more turns of thread.

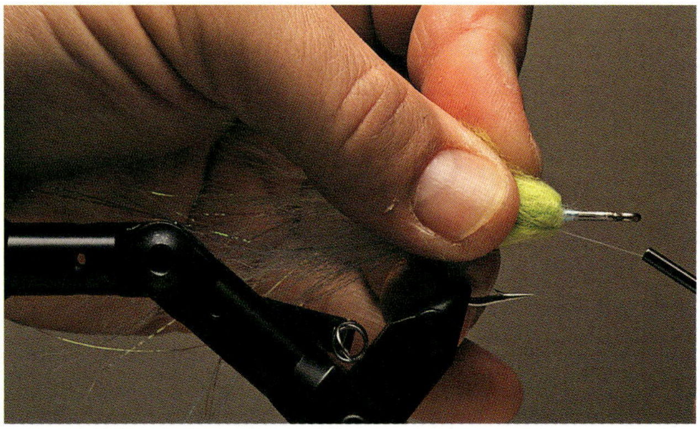

16. Holding the fleece back tightly, work the thread forward . . .

17. . . . until it is again in front of the fleece.

18. Pick out the fleece with the point of your bodkin This important step will ensure that the fleece is tangle free and smooth when trimmed and ready to be coated with the silicone.

19. Repeat steps 11 through 18 until the shank of the hook is filled with fleece. Wrap several additional turns of thread and tie off just behind the hook eye.

20. It is very important that you begin trimming by making the bottom cut first. Long-bladed scissors give better control when making this first cut. Note that this cut is close to the hook shank, so more material will be left above than below the hook shank. This will retain the hook gape and contribute to the balance and behavior of the fly.

After you make your first cut, picture the outline of the bait to guide you in trimming the rest of the fleece.

21. The first cut is completed. From this point, you can envision the shape the mullet head will take.

22. Continue trimming the head to the desired shape—oval, round, triangular, whatever—while leaving the veil from the first wrap extending over the bucktail. Note how the bucktail "shoulders" tied in earlier and the fleece veil contribute to the fly's symmetry.

23. Top view of the trimmed fly, prior to application of silicone.

24. Use two applications of silicone. A good base coat is important, so don't make it too thin. The second coat can be somewhat thinner. To apply the first coat, dab silicone on the fleece with your fingertip, starting at the front.

25. Spread it evenly over the entire trimmed fleece body, making sure all the fleece tips are covered to a smooth finish. This first dollop will generally not be sufficient to cover the entire fleece head. You will have to add small dollops successively as you go. Feather the silicone coating toward the rear with light strokes of your fingertip, as if trying to wipe it off your finger. Thin out the material as you work toward the rear, so that the ends of the longer fleece fibers of the veil have no silicone on them. Make sure to seal the front of the fly well around the hook eye to keep out water.

26. A small plastic knife helps to reach underneath the body, especially for smaller flies.

27. Once the first coat is set, perhaps ten minutes, add prism eyes.

28. Apply four dollops of silicone for the second coat, over the eyes, on the top, and on the bottom.

29. Spread the final coat of silicone as the first, but be sure to use a wetting agent to spread the silicone smoothly and leave a slick finish. Notice the finger moistened with Photo-Flo solution. Try patting or pressing the silicone gently around the eyes, rather than stroking it, to keep from moving the eyes.

30. Add final strokes with the knife. It helps to dip the knife blade in the Photo-Flo solution too.

31. The finished Siliclone Mullet, shown actual size.

32. Finished Siliclone Mullet, top view.

Here are some additional tying tips that will help you produce better Siliclones:

Use good-quality fleece of a medium soft texture. Ram's wool or sheep fleece that is very wiry or stiff will make it more difficult to achieve a smoothly trimmed and finished head. Note, too, the puffiness of the fleece. The air trapped in the silicone sheath contributes to the spongy texture of the fly as well as the buoyancy. The thickness of the silicone must be judged from practice. There are several variables, like size and fleece texture, that make it difficult to instruct exactly how much to use or how thick it should be. Notice also that the hook is more toward the bottom of the fleece, not in the center.

You can control the shape of the fly body, whether oval or round, as well as the size, by the way you trim with your scissors.

Use a hook with a wide gap for this fly, preferably with a Model Perfect bend, like those made by Partridge (Homosassa Special) and Owner. If you use a hook like the Tiemco 800S, which has a slightly turned-in drop point, use one size larger, to maintain the gape.

This cutaway shows the air pockets in the fleece, which give the fly buoyancy. Keeping most of the fleece above the hook shank gives better balance and action to the fly, as well as a larger gape.

Make the fly thinner and don't carry the silicone as far to the rear if you want it to sink more readily.

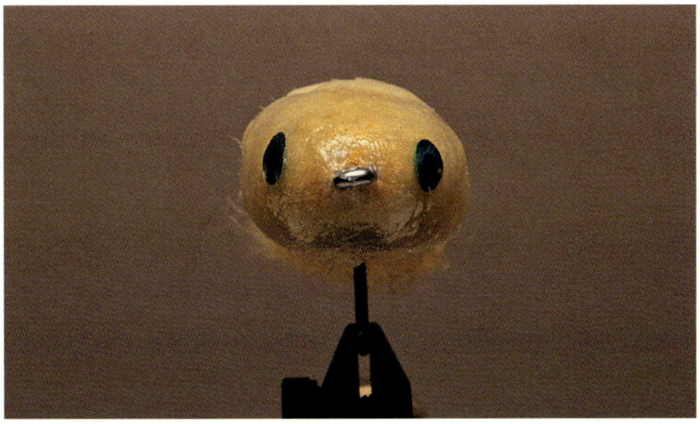

A large, oval-head Siliclone.

A small, cylindrical Siliclone.

Take pains to tie and pack the fleece tightly and trim it smoothly, preferably to the texture of velour. If these steps are not done carefully, the silicone will not hide gaps or bumps in the fleece, but rather accentuate them. The Siliclone is repairable. If the fly tears or is bitten by a fish, smear silicone over the cut. It's as convenient as repairing a puncture in neoprene waders.

As we recommended when discussing epoxy flies, experiment, using the Siliclone procedures outlined above, to create imitations of other baits. In addition to the simple design given here, we variously incorporate ostrich herl, saddle hackles, rattles, and flexible rubber legs into our Siliclones to produce different actions, movements, and effects. Starting from the original mullet pattern, we have produced effective menhaden, eel, and mackerel patterns, as well as bluegills, snakes, frogs, and mice for freshwater versions. The Siliclone is a good pattern on which to exercise your ingenuity and creativity.

Fishing Tip: Fishing Siliclones

Siliclones are great to fish over submerged weeds and snags. They swim shallow and can be made to float back to the top on the pause, avoiding hangups. Or you can fish them above rocky structure by using a sinking line and short leader. The fly will stay down but resist hanging up on the bottom because of its natural buoyancy.

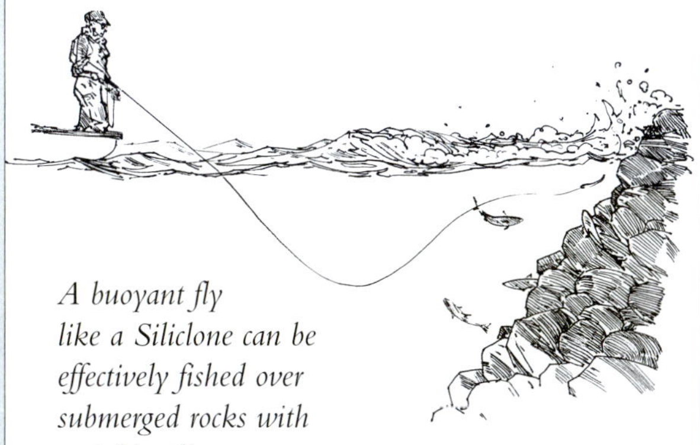

A buoyant fly like a Siliclone can be effectively fished over submerged rocks with a sinking line.

Siliclones are especially productive when you splat them down hard in the whitewater around jetties.

POP LIPS

Surf casters have always had great success with swimming plugs like the Atom, Redfin, Bomber, Danny, Gibbs Swimmer, Creek Chub Darter, and such, especially when fishing for striped bass, bluefish, and channel bass. Fly casters, by contrast, had always experienced frustration in trying to match the wobbling and swimming motion of these plugs by using traditional and conventional fly patterns. Most of the hard-bodied lures incorporated a lip, which enabled them to achieve their enticing motion.

Some tiers attempted to create swimming flies by adding lips of lacquered deer hair, adding hard, curved sections of plastic cut from plastic drinking cups, artificial fingernails, and other sources. None proved satisfactory to us, and none ever gained wide acceptance. Here's how the lipped, swimming version of the Siliclone evolved.

Bob called me one day and asked, "What do we really need in a saltwater fly?" I answered, "For years I've been toying with the idea of a swimming fly. Not one with long, wavy hackles or marabou, but a creation that actually swims, like a Redfin or Bomber or one of the other casting and spinning plugs. I just haven't come up with anything practical." Within a couple of days, Bob called with the announcement that he had such a fly. Incredulous after so many experimental failures, I drove the 100 miles to see this imagined solution. Only it wasn't imagined. The first lipped Siliclone swam more actively and enticingly than I had imagined possible. Bob had simply taken the next logical step. The Siliclone was already an accepted member of the Pop Fleyes family; it seemed simple enough to incorporate some of the same material and technique to give the fly an integrated lip. It was crude, but the direction was right on.

The Siliclone technique has made true swimming flies practical. The Pop Lip is not a show piece, a tying *tour de force*. It is a practical solution to a defined problem, a concept turned to realization. It has built-in action. No additional rod work or line manipulation is required. All the action comes from the fly design itself. Simply pull it in a straight line through the water, and the fly will swing and wiggle side to side. Some purists feel, and indeed have stated emphatically, that a fly should not possess inherent action and that all motion should come from the angler's manipulation of rod and line. They are certainly entitled to their views, but it seems that feathers, like marabou, and hair, like rabbit, already give natural action to a fly, and these are widely accepted. We offer the same reply to those who reject

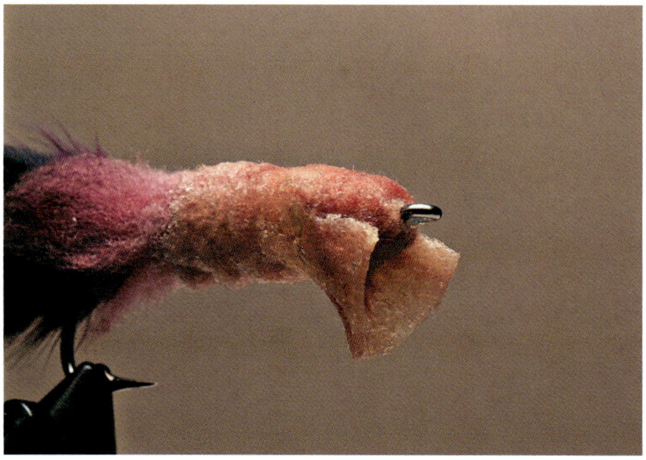

The first Pop Lip attempt. It was crude and tricky to shape the lip, but it laid the foundation for further development.

A second-generation fly, only slightly improved. The red fleece was needed to keep track of the lip so it wasn't trimmed away.

lead eyes, cone heads, and plastic tails: Simply don't use them if they offend your fly-fishing and fly-tying ethic. We and most anglers we know are thrilled with swimming and jigging flies, which add so much to our sport.

The technique we now use, which is illustrated below, is a vast improvement over the earliest versions we showed and practiced years ago. This technique is simpler and more tier friendly: the results are also more predictable. As with epoxy Surf Candies, the key to this fly is in handling and manipulating the material. The Pop Lip is one of the best examples of constant refinement in fly design.

Siliclone Pop Lip

Materials

Heavy model perfect hook, Partridge Homosassa or similar style
Fine monofilament thread
Bucktail
Sheep fleece or ram's wool
Wire brush or comb
Clear silicone
Kodak Photo-Flo solution
Self-sticking prism eyes

1. Build a Siliclone as previously described, but instead of filling the hook shank with fleece before trimming, leave just enough space behind the hook eye for one more tie of fleece. Now trim the fleece as shown above, before adding the last tie of fleece.

2. Prepare the final tuft of sheep fleece, and push it over the front of the fly with your tying hand, spreading it 360 degrees around the shank. Transfer the fleece to your materials hand and catch it with two loose wraps of thread. It will help in constructing the lip to leave a little more fleece to the front, with just enough to the rear of the thread to grasp with the fingers of your materials hand.

3. Catch the material with two loose wraps, then tie down the fleece securely. Note that the hook eye is covered at this point.

4. The interlocking fibers of fleece require you to manually expose the hook eye, so with your tying hand, pull all the fleece that is in front around to the underside of the shank and force the hook eye through the network of fleece.

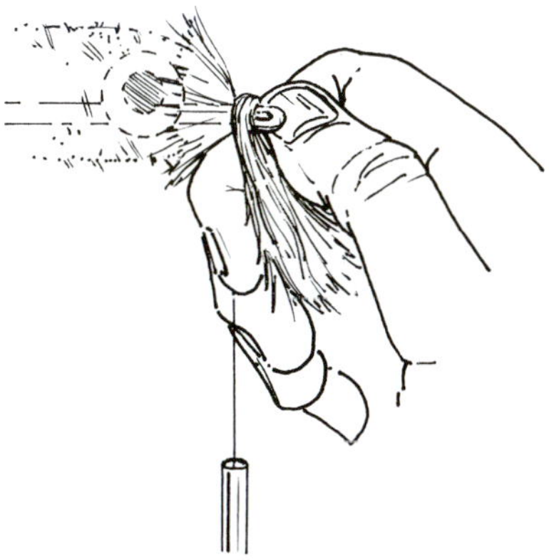

Pull the lip fleece down firmly below the hook with your tying hand.

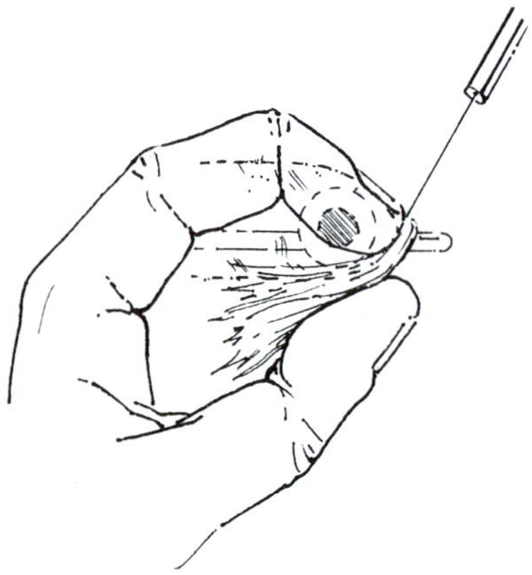

Hold the fleece in place with your materials hand while working the thread forward through the fleece with your tying hand.

5. Once the eye is through the fleece, release the fleece in your tying hand, grab the bobbin, and raise it straight up over the fly. Now, with your materials hand, pull all the fleece to the rear tightly. Bring the thread forward, make several wraps just behind the hook eye, and tie off. The thread must be wrapped tightly against the fleece before letting go to ensure that it stays in place. As with many tying operations, this is more difficult to describe in words than it is to perform.

6. The lip, resembling a beard or bib, will be formed from the fleece on the bottom, in front of the fly. Note that the eye of the hook is not visible here only because of the angle of the photograph.

7. Trim away all excess above and behind the lip.

8. Top view. Note that the eye is free and clear.

9. Front view. The fibers extend over more than a 180-degree radius, reaching up to approximately 10:00 and 2:00.

10. Start the initial trimming by cutting the tips of the fleece away. This will provide a rough guide to the lip outline. Work gradually with your scissors, progressively eliminating corners and angles until the lip approaches a round shape.

11. Front view of lip completely trimmed prior to application of silicone and final trimming. You don't need a lot of fleece for the lip. We imagine the hair rather like reinforcing rods in concrete. Its principal function is to provide a foundation to hold the silicone. A lip that is too thick will be difficult to work with and lose flexibility once it is coated with silicone.

12. Put a dollop of silicone on your fingertip and thumb. Squeeze them together over the fleece so that the silicone equally coats the front and back of the fleece at the same time. Be sure always to stroke the silicone in the direction of the fibers. Don't pull all the fibers downward.

13. Final trimming now takes place. As when roughly shaping the dry lip, trim progressively. Cut the lip square, and eliminate corners and angles until the lip is round. It should be a bit wider than the widest part of the head and not as deep as the gape of the hook.

14. Front view of the finished lip.

15. Side view of the finished Pop Lips Siliclone, after a) the silicone has been applied to the whole head, b) eyes have been put in place, and c) the second application of silicone, all as described above for the simple Siliclone. (Actual size, $4^{7}/_{8}$ inches)

16. Finished Pop Lip, top view.

17. Simple Siliclone and Pop Lip, showing the family resemblance in the two versions.

Additional tips about the Pop Lip:

There are many variables in the composition of this fly. Before fishing with a Pop Lip, test it on the water. Since each is an individual creation and not mass produced, each will swim slightly differently. Some cut a wider swath; others wiggle more tightly. You can control this by the angle, size, and shape of the lip, as well as the size of the fly and weight of the hook. We often leave the lip a little larger than desired but carry a small pair of scissors with us to trim the lip and fine-tune the fly if needed while fishing. That is why we strongly urge you to experiment and get familiar with the material and its potential.

It's important to appreciate the critical keel action of the hook. As rule, a large lip is better for quieter waters and weaker currents. A lip that is too large or too wide and powerful, however, may overcome the hook's effect and cause the fly to spin. A smaller lip will diminish the side-to-side movement, and the fly will have shorter, quicker action, which is better suited to stronger currents and faster retrieves. Especially, make certain that the lip does not protrude down lower than the hook point, for this is likely to inhibit or disrupt the swimming action.

When you store lip flies, be careful not to crush them or place anything heavy on them. Distorting the shape of the lip will ruin the action.

Carry a small pair of scissors for fine-tuning the Pop Lip on the water to modify its motion.

When retrieved, a properly tied and trimmed Pop Lip fly will swim side to side like a plastic-lipped plug.

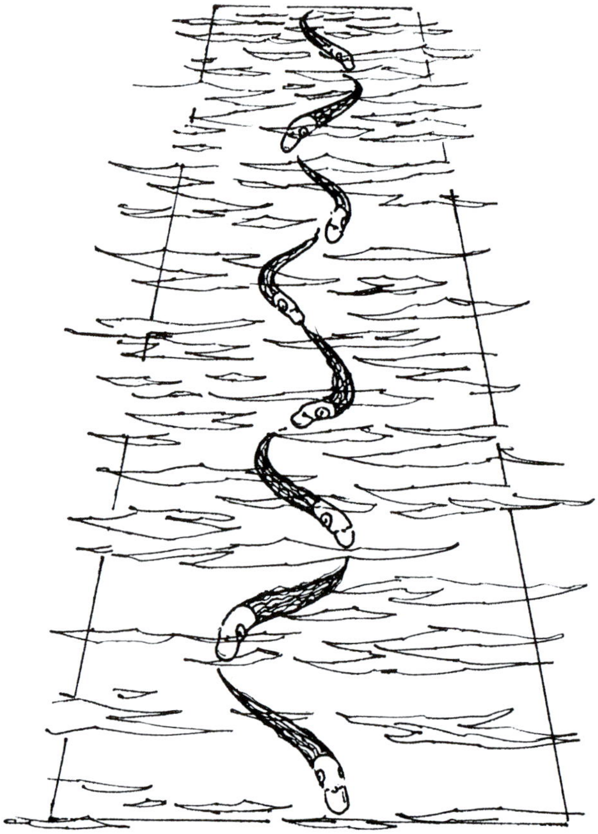

Full Dress Pop Lip

Here is a version incorporating ostrich herl and saddle hackles, in addition to the bucktail, plus greater length. It has a much more snaky swimming motion than the simple version shown above. The head actually swings back and forth several inches, while the long herl and hackles trace sweeping S curves behind it. Additionally, we colored the top of the fleece yellow with a permanent marker to harmonize with the hair and feathers and to give a two-tone contrast to the fly. There is no need to use two different colors of fleece. This particular color fly was constructed to mimic the look and action of a yellow and white Bomber plug, one of the east coast's most highly successful striped bass lures.

Begin by tying in a single bunch of white bucktail at the bend of the hook, as for any Siliclone fly, but make the hair more sparse than normal to allow for the addition of the other materials.

Add a bunch of yellow ostrich herl, about three times the length of the hook shank, on top of the bucktail.

Add six yellow saddle hackles slightly longer than the herl. Tie them in "clock fashion," one at a time, as per the instructions for the Semper Fleye (page 105).

Proceed with the fleece, silicone, and lip as described for the Siliclone and Pop Lip.

Materials

Heavy model perfect hook, Partridge Homosassa or similar style
Fine monofilament thread
Bucktail
Sheep fleece or ram's wool
Wire brush or comb
Clear silicone
Kodak Photo-Flo solution
Self-sticking prism eyes
Ostrich herl
Saddle hackles

A Full Dress Pop Lip with ostrich herl and saddle hackles for more action. (Actual size, 6 1/4 inches)

The lip produces the erratic swimming action of the Pop Lip.

The two-tone effect is produced with a yellow permanent felt-tip marker.

The Full Dress Pop Lip has as much built-in action as a Bomber, one of the top striped bass plugs on the east coast.

Fishing Tip: Fishing the Pop Lip

The Pop Lip works best if you attach it to your leader using the nonslip mono loop knot described for Jiggy flies (page 53). Any knot that tightens around the wire of the hook eye inhibits the fly's in-built swimming motion.

Also, we highly recommend that you employ a two-handed retrieve. Using a standard strip with only your line hand causes the fly to alternately stop and go. While this is often an excellent retrieve for some flies, you will get your best results out of the Pop Lip if you keep it steadily swimming. When the fly lands, simply place the rod under one arm, and with the rod tip pointing directly at the fly, pull the line slowly and steadily, hand over hand. And don't worry about hooking up. Simply continue to pull the line hard and fast when a fish takes. You will actually get better hookups without having to allow for the flex of the rod. Whether you use a one-handed or two-hand retrieve, line management is important. You can let the line fall onto the ground or the floor of the boat, but a stripping basket, either worn around the waist or free-standing between your feet, will minimize tangles and keep you from stepping on the line.

Finally, this fly swims best when the current is not too strong nor the water too turbulent. You will get optimum performance in stillwater or in a slow, steady current.

This striped bass was pulled from the jetty rocks by a white Pop Lip.

A bluefish mistook a yellow Pop Lip swimming over a sandbar for the real thing.

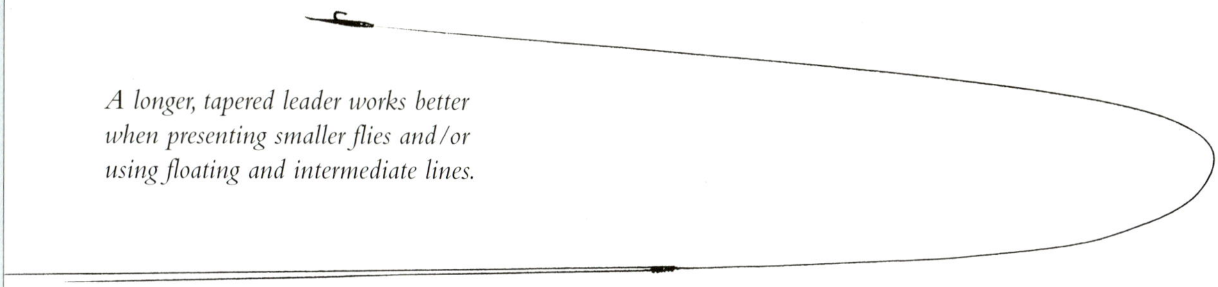

A longer, tapered leader works better when presenting smaller flies and/or using floating and intermediate lines.

Use a shorter, heavier leader with little or no taper when fishing larger and heavier flies like Siliclones and/or when fishing fast-sinking lines.

A stripping basket is an indispensable accessory for fishing swimming flies in the surf.

WEEDLESS SILICLONES

Some fishing conditions call for flies that are highly snag and weed resistant. We have written about and used at least a dozen different techniques for constructing flies that avoid hangups, from simple upside-down flies, like Clousers and Gotchas, to elaborate mono and wire weed guards. Various solutions work more or less effectively with different flies and under different conditions. If you want to fish a surface fly-rod lure in heavily obstructed waters such as mangrove creeks, or when floating eel-grass, especially common during times of spring tides, presents a major problem, use the Weedless Bendback Siliclone. Fishing from a jetty along New Jersey's Barnegat Inlet, we have caught false albacore on this fly amid heavy floating grass. This would have been virtually impossible with conventional fly designs. We also tested this design thoroughly in heavily weed-infested waters while fishing for northern pike on several trips to Saskatchewan. It's possible to dance and flip the Weedless Siliclone through lily pads, weeds, grass, and timber stickups and never hang up. It is easily the most weedless fly we have ever used. Working it through heavy grass and weeds is akin to dancing a cigar-shaped Zara Spook plug, with the treble hooks removed. Even in extreme situations, like the pike fishing we did, the only hangups were caused by the wire leaders we had to use, which sometimes caught in the notches of the lily pads.

Weedlesss Bendback Siliclone

The Weedless Bendback Siliclone is simple to tie, and if you have tried tying the simple Siliclone, you already know all you need to know and have the materials called for. This fly requires only a slightly different application.

Materials

Heavy model perfect hook, Partridge Homosassa or similar style
Fine monofilament thread
Bucktail
Sheep fleece or ram's wool
Wire brush or comb
Clear silicone
Kodak Photo-Flo solution
Self-sticking prism eyes

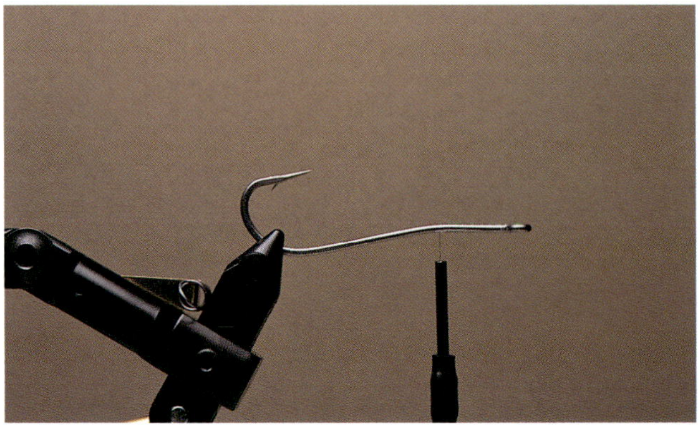

1. Slightly bend a long-shank hook, in this case a Tiemco 2/0 911S, into a bendback shape (see page 50). Attach and position your thread as shown.

2. Attach a fairly full bunch of bucktail, about one and a half times the length of the hook, at the bend in the shank.

3. Attach a long, thin "spike" of bucktail on top of this. It is not necessary to use a contrasting color as shown, but it here illustrates the amount of topmost hairs needed for the weed guard.

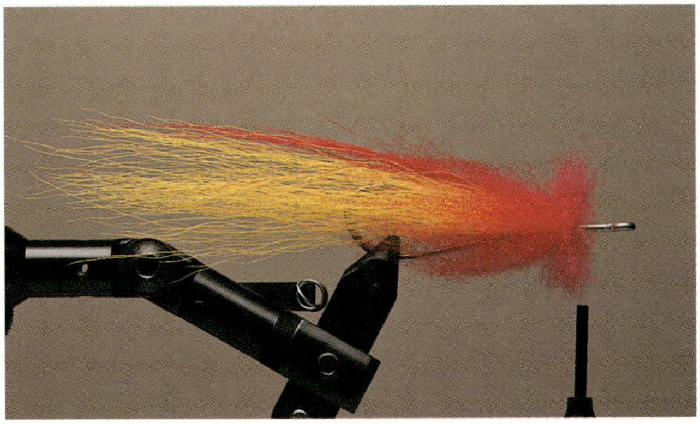

4. Attach the first tuft of sheep fleece, tips rearward, as described for the regular Siliclone.

5. Fill the hook shank with successive bunches of fleece.

6. Trim the fleece as for the regular Siliclone.

7. Coat the spike of bucktail, saturating it well with silicone. This will be used for fashioning the weed guard.

8. After giving all the fleece two applications of silicone, with eyes added after the first coat, reinforce the weed guard spike with additional silicone.

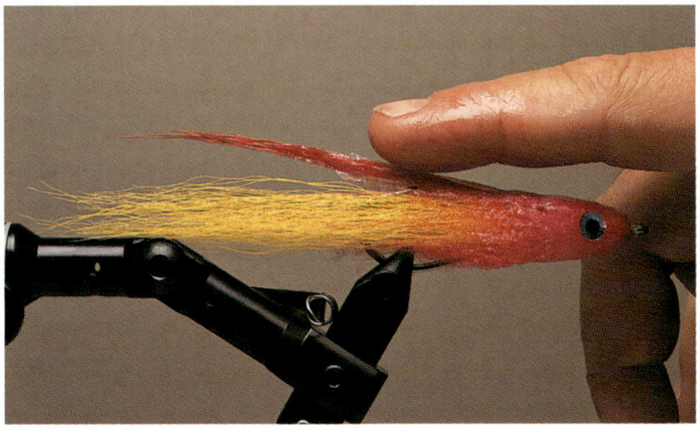

9. Blend the silicone so that the weed guard extends smoothly from the head, with no gaps.

10. After the silicone is cured, preferably overnight, snip off the spike just beyond the hook point.

11. The finished Weedless Bendback Siliclone, after a few final snips to neaten the weed guard. The short weed guard is firm enough to resist pressure from sticks and weeds but readily yields to pressure from almost any fish's mouth. (Fly shown actual size.)

Rubber Candy

This recalls the epoxy Surf Candy described in the previous chapter but marries the concept of the Surf Candy with some of the features of the Siliclone. It achieves much of the realism and durability of the epoxy Surf Candy, but with less weight. It also behaves slightly differently in the water due to the buoyancy of the material. This fly has a subtle body semitranslucence and glow, achieved by the underbody flash showing through silicone. This has been a good fly for false albacore and other tunas, as well as striped bass.

Materials

Standard-length saltwater hook
Fine monofilament thread
Bucktail
Ostrich herl
Cactus Chenille or Estaz
Clear silicone
Self-sticking prism eyes

1. Starting with the thread at the bend of the hook, tie in a medium-size bunch of bucktail hairs, two to three times the hook length, and fasten down securely.

2. Add pearl Flashabou or other flash over bucktail.

3. Add some olive ostrich herl, the same length as the bucktail, on top.

4. Attach a length of Estaz, Cactus Chenille, or other braided flash at the bend.

5. Wrap the Estaz forward and tie it off behind the eye.

6. Trim the ends off the braided flash material, tapering down toward the front of the fly.

7. Add more ostrich herl over the whole, tied down at the front, behind the eye, and tie off the thread.

8. Apply the first coat of silicone over the body, back as far as the hook bend. Be sure to saturate all the materials well, working silicone in between all the fibers, herl, and flash.

9. Add prism eyes.

10. Apply the finish coat of silicone over the whole body, as far as the hook bend.

11. Smooth out the silicone, using Photo-Flo, as described for the simple Siliclone, and the Rubber Candy is finished. (Fly shown actual size.)

Rubber Squid

As we said when discussing the Candy Squid in the previous chapter, epoxy is not the most convenient material for larger squid imitations. Beyond a certain point, it's too difficult to work with and makes a fly too heavy. Not so for silicone, which is easier for most tiers to work with. Here is a simple, easy-to-make squid imitation that is eminently castable and interprets a squid with sufficient realism. Utilizing the opaque nature of a film of silicone and an Estaz underglow, as in the Rubber Candy, you can give this fly a ghostlike glow in the water.

Materials

Long-shank saltwater hook
Fine monofilament thread
Bucktail
Ostrich herl
Cactus Chenille or Estaz
Clear silicone
Self-sticking prism eyes

1. Attach pearl Estaz at bend of the hook.

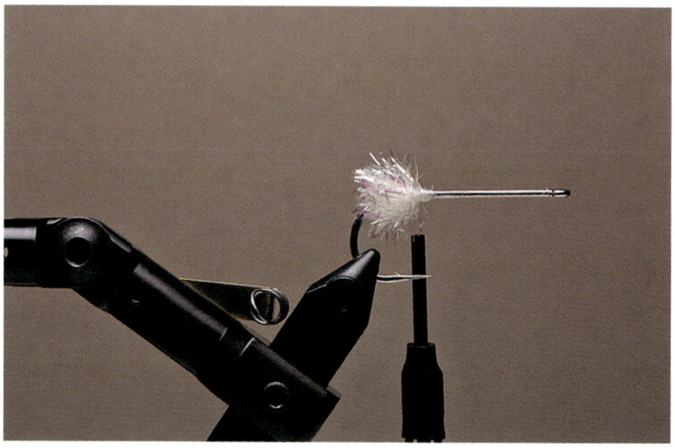

2. Wrap just a few turns tightly to create a small ball of material and tie it off. This ball will keep the tentacles apart on the finished fly.

3. Add up to a dozen pieces of ostrich herl, a little longer than the hook, evenly distributed around the shank.

4. Wrap the shank, back to front, with the Estaz and trim the tip with your scissors, tapering the material down toward the hook eye.

5. Apply the first coat of silicone as described above for other silicone flies. Saturate the material to the hook shank as much as possible.

6. Add eyes and a second application of silicone. (Fly shown actual size.)

Silicone Squid

Here is a classic example of a fly that incorporates more than one Pop Fleye technique. This fly is in reality a version of the Shady Lady Squid, which is partly tied between two vises (see page 114–118), given a silicone treatment. This squid, complete with plastic legs and fins, uses silicone over fleece in a completely different manner from the Siliclone flies. Instead of packing fleece in tight bunches, as we do for the Siliclone, we create a hollow sheath around the body.

Materials

Standard-length saltwater hook
Fine monofilament thread
Bucktail
Ostrich herl
Cactus Chenille or Estaz
Clear silicone
Self-sticking prism eyes
Sheep fleece or ram's wool
Rubber Sililegs

1. Begin with a partially completed Shady Lady Squid (p. 116–118) but one tied with Sililegs tentacles (see page 64).

2. Tie a veil of fleece at the hook eye so that the fibers are distributed around the body, reaching past the eyes, and with the butt ends sticking out well past the hook eye, as shown.

3. Apply a light coat of silicone over the fleece, and trim the tips from around the head of the squid so the eyes are exposed. The body should feel like a hollow tube—that is, when you lightly squeeze it, it compresses and then springs back into shape.

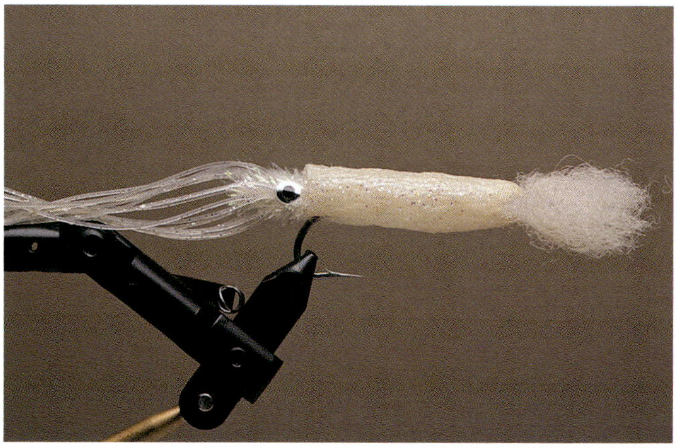

4. Pull all the butt ends of the fleece down and spread them to the sides of the hook eye. Don't cut off this material, as it will be used to fashion the swim fins.

5. Trim the ends of the fleece fibers in an arc, as shown here with the vise rotated.

6. Spread silicone over the fin fleece, shown here from side and top.

7. Trim the ends of the fin fleece.

8. Now, fold the fin material forward onto the top of the body and coat the entire body and fins with another coat of silicone.

9. Side view of squid with fins. (Fly shown actual size.)

10. Top view of fins after final trimming.

Wiggle Siliclone

Here is another creation, similar to the epoxy Wiggle Candies shown in the previous chapter, which some traditionalists have trouble accepting. They feel it is not a true fly and that we might as well use the entire plastic bait. The option is theirs to use or ignore. We are simply exploring potential directions in fly tying. Be that as it may, we have found it a practical and effective lure. The example shown here incorporates a section from a commercially available lure called a Redgill. You can also use a Flexi Tail, Twister Tail, or Fin S Fish and achieve slightly different action.

Materials

Standard-length or short-shank saltwater hook
Fine monofilament thread
Bucktail
Sheep fleece or ram's wool
Wire brush or comb
Clear silicone
Kodak Photo-Flo solution
Self-sticking prism eyes
Redgill lure

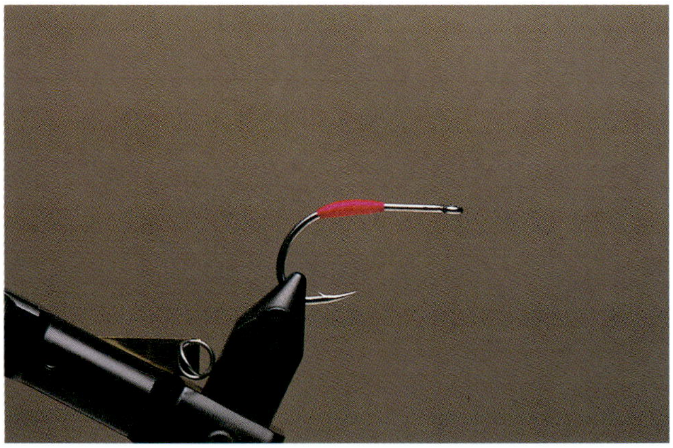

1. Near the bend of a short-shank hook, build a small mound with any tying floss available. The color is unimportant, as it will be covered. We use red here only for illustration purposes.

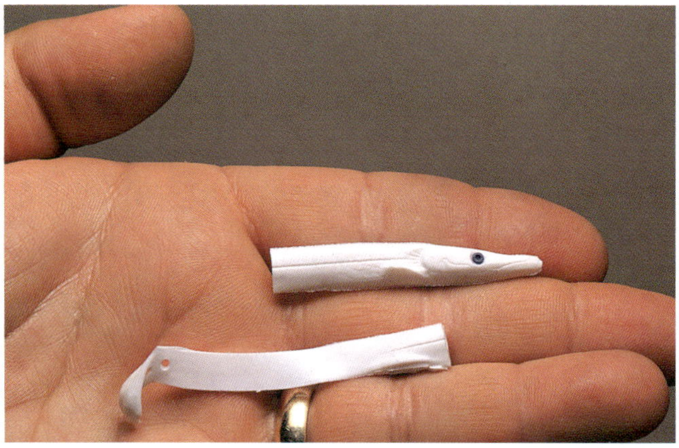

2. Cut a Redgill soft plastic bait in half.

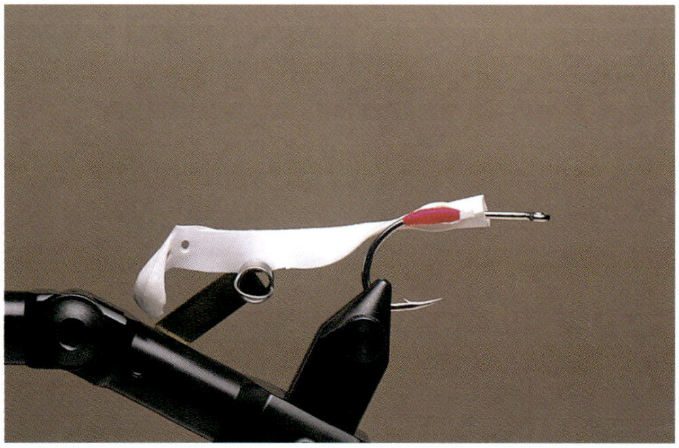

3. Slip the tail over the hook by inserting the eye into the vent and sliding the tail section to the bend. The tail is turned here simply to show how the hook fits into it.

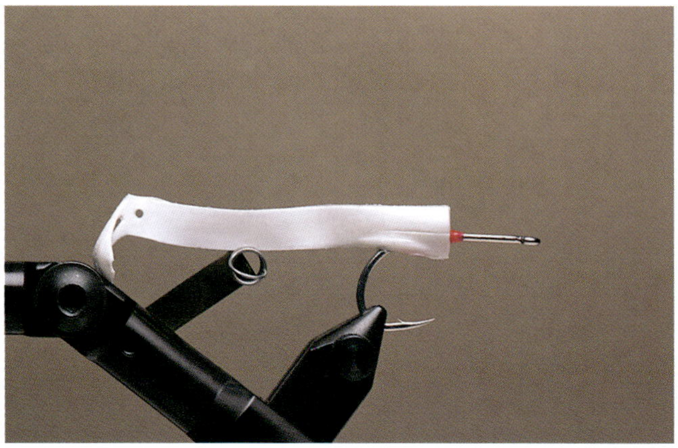

4. Put a drop of Krazy Glue or other cyanoacrylate on the floss. Straighten the tail section, slide it to the bend as shown, and hold it in place for a few seconds while the glue sets.

5. Attach a couple of successive bunches of fleece to the hook shank as described above for the regular Siliclone.

6. Trim the fleece, coat with silicone, add eyes, and give it a second coating of silicone.

Fishing Tip: Leaders

Long, fine leaders may be necessary when casting to spooky bonefish, but they make presentation and casting difficult when fishing large and heavy flies, such as Siliclones and some large flies to be shown later. Your cast may transport the fly, but the leader may not turn it over. Make your leaders shorter and heavier throughout, 5 to 7 feet long for surface and intermediate lines, and tapered from no more than two or three sections. When using fast-sinking lines or shooting tapers, we generally use a single piece of medium stiff 20- or 30-pound-test monofilament or fluorocarbon, between 1 1/2 and 3 feet long.

Chapter Five

Additional Pop Fleye Designs

This chapter catalogs a variety of designs not employing epoxy or silicone, except as possible options or in the subtlest ways. Some of these creations will appeal to more traditional-minded tiers. Within this potpourri of designs, you will sometimes find a simple variation on a theme, a novel twist, a new use of some traditional material, or some new material or technique to be incorporated with other ideas, as opposed to a completely new fly design.

3D FLIES

Sculpting flies, shaping fly bodies from one or occasionally two principal tying materials—that is what 3D and other flies modeled on them are all about. The aim here is to capture the subtle, natural curves and lines of baitfish, thicker in some places, thinner in others, with tapers on top, bottom, sides, front, and rear. The finished flies have the shape and even the feel of natural baits. If you close your eyes, hold a 3D in one hand and a natural

LEFTY KREH

bait in the other, then squeeze them, they feel amazingly similar. Because, of their three-dimensional look and feel, Lefty Kreh called the early samples he saw 3D flies, and the name has stuck.

We first gave instructions for tying a 3D in the August 1993 issue of *Salt Water Fly Fishing* magazine. Although these flies may take a little more time, they are simple in concept and not really difficult at all, but they will train you in effective scissor work better than any other fly type. The technique results in flies that are very personal and individual. It is creativity turned loose. Forming 3D's involves two procedures: first, layering or stacking UltraHair or Super Hair in specific areas on the hook shank, and second, trimming it to shape with deft scissor work. In principle, it is a lot like trimming spun deer hair or fleece, as discussed for the Siliclone, even akin to trimming a bonsai tree. Picture in your mind the finished product, then make minute snips and cuts here and there, using mostly the scissor tips, working at the front, then the sides and rear of the fly.

When creating a 3D, consider the thickness, slope, shape, silhouette, outline, and especially the tapers of the natural you are imitating. Note that many baitfish are thicker in the back or shoulder area, thinner in the belly. Viewed head on, a 3D tapers top to bottom. From the top and side, it tapers front to rear. Since the tying involves much stacking and layering of hair, you may need a little practice to get the feel of just how much hair to use for each tie in, and this will be determined by the fullness you want your bait to have.

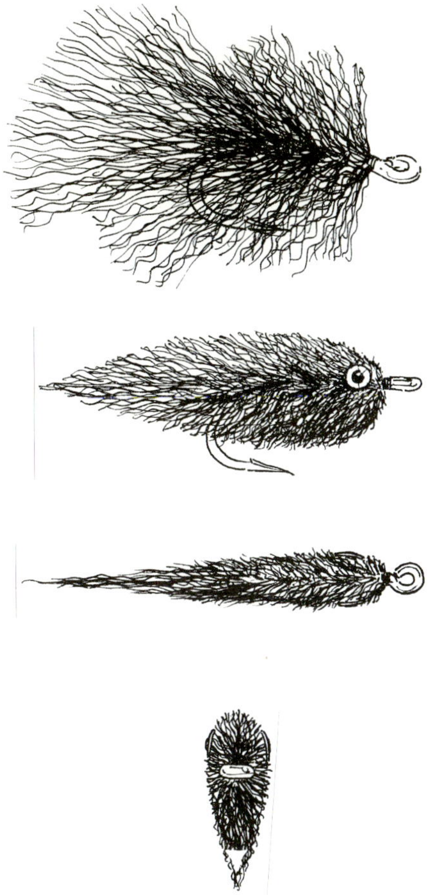

Trim the 3D fly so that it reveals tapers from the side (front to back), the top (front to back), and the front (top to bottom), similar to a natural baitfish.

3D Baitfish

Materials
Standard-length saltwater hook
UltraHair or Super Hair
Fine monofilament thread
Pearl Polar Flash or Flashabou
Prism eyes

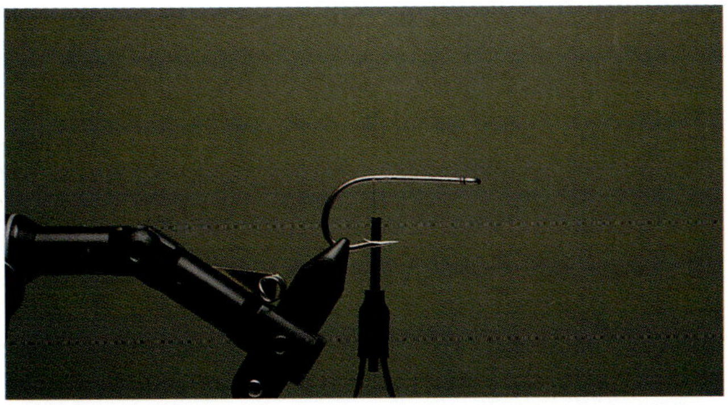

1. Start with the thread attached near the bend of the hook, in this case a 4/0 Tiemco 800S.

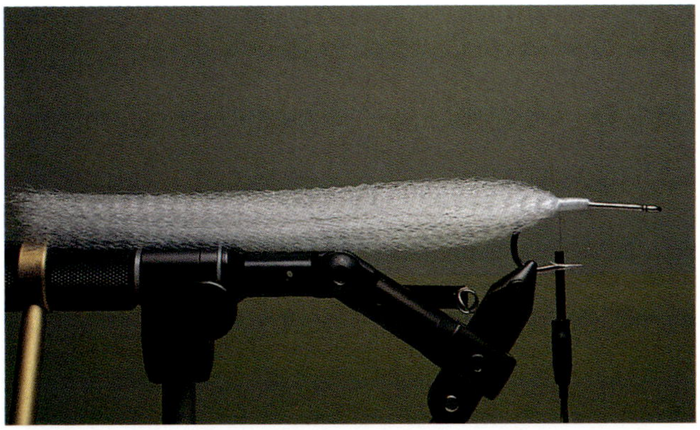

2. Tie in a length of UltraHair, spread around the hook.

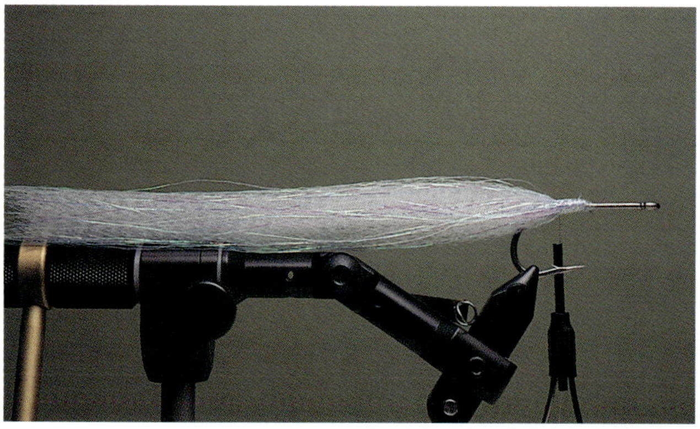

3. Add a sparse layer of pearl Polar Flash distributed evenly around the fly.

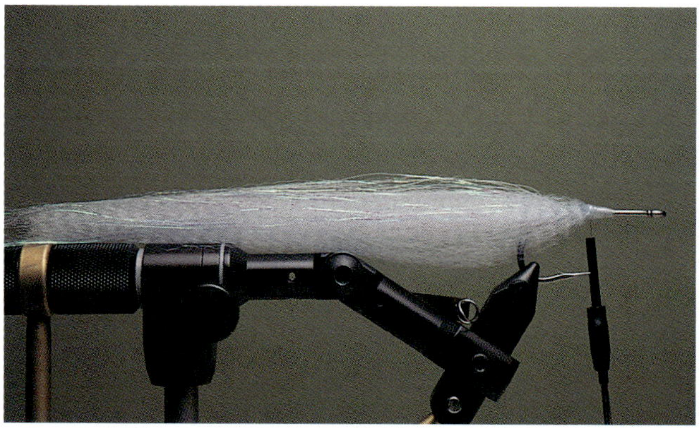

4. Tie in a shorter length of hair underneath to be used for forming the belly.

5. Add more flash.

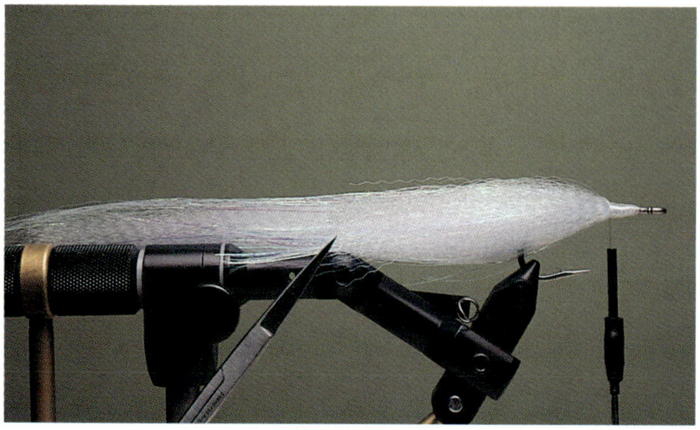

6. Tie in some UltraHair along the sides to form "shoulders" for the baitfish. The scissors points to the end of the side hairs, indicating the ends of the hair lengths.

7. Here the fly is turned to show the shoulders.

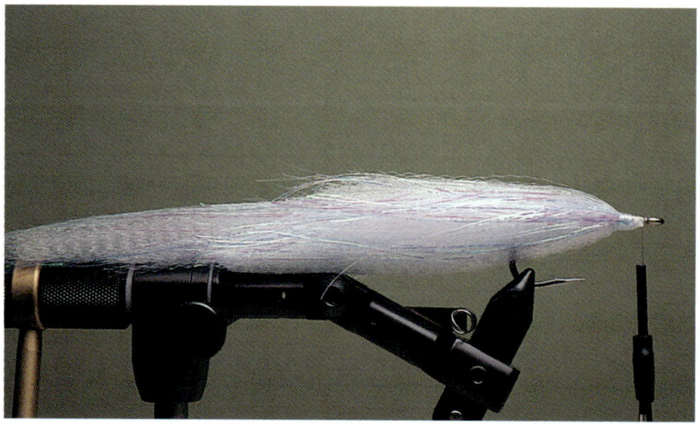

8. Again, a little more flash has been added.

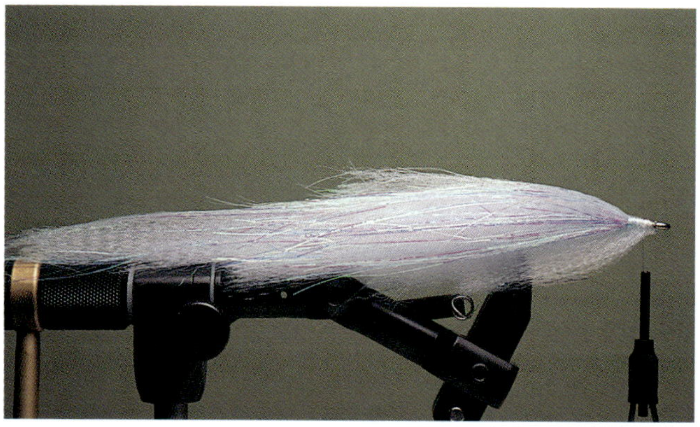

9. Add a bunch of hair to the belly of the fly.

10. Add more hair to the top of the fly, and tie off the thread. Your fly may require the addition of even more hair, depending on size and hook length.

11. The untrimmed 3D.

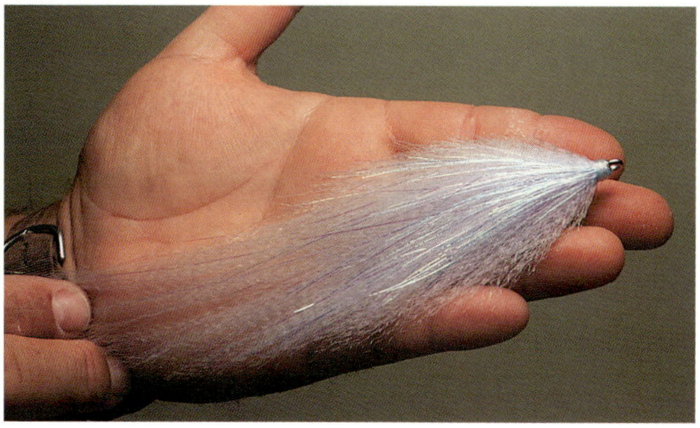

12. The 3D trimmed top, sides, and bottom. Trim gradually, with short cutting strokes from the back and side, using mainly the scissor points, then finish with some longer cuts from front to rear to finish the shape.

13. The finished 3D with eyes attached, using a spot of Krazy Glue, and head wraps coated with head cement. Since the hair is packed so tightly and the hair ends are all trimmed shorter toward the front of the fly, it is virtually nonfouling. (Actual size, 7 inches)

3D Squid

By distributing the hair evenly around the body and using rubber Sililegs, you can fashion an effective small squid imitation round in cross section. (Actual size, 3 inches)

Bucktail Deceiver

This fly takes its inspiration from Lefty's Deceiver, the most traditional and popular of all saltwater flies, the fly that represents the first modern step in saltwater design. Again, this is not so much novel design as it is a different way of approaching a traditional idea. It employs traditional materials in a slightly unconventional application, using the thinking employed in the 3D. The Bucktail Deceiver produces the same overall shape as Lefty's Deceiver but with more roundness, fullness, buoyancy, and a slightly different behavior in the water. The entire fly is constructed of bucktail, so the tapering and silhouette are achieved from the natural tapering of the material and its careful placement, rather than formed by extensive scissor work. While this design eliminates the search for expensive, quality hackles, size is limited to the length of the bucktail you can procure. The Bucktail Deceiver does not replace the traditional version, but explores and expands its potential, offering an optional design.

Materials

Tiemco 911S or other long-shank hook
Fine monofilament thread
Bucktail, longest available
Self-sticking prism eyes

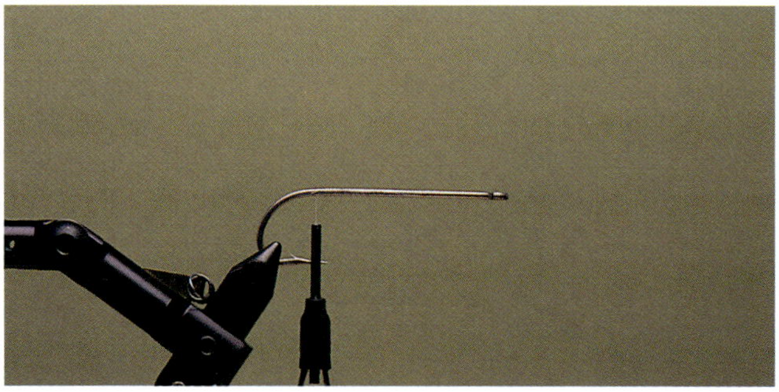

1. Start with the thread at the bend of a long-shank hook, here a 4/0 Tiemco 911S.

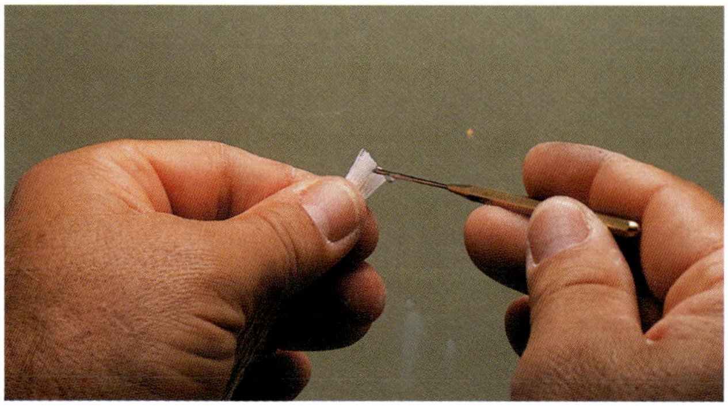

2. Cut a medium bunch of very long bucktail. With your bodkin, force some head cement into the butt ends for durability in the finished fly.

3. Attach the bucktail at the bend. It is two to three times the hook length. Spread the hair fibers around the shank, not just on top.

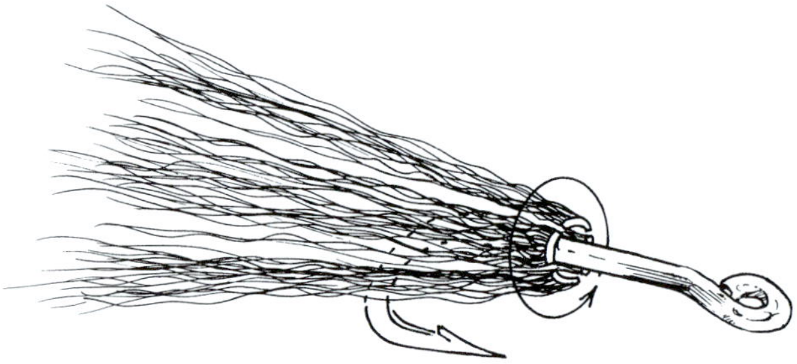

Distribute each bunch of bucktail evenly around the hook shank.

4. Tie a light veil of flash, in this case pearl Flashabou, over the bucktail, spread all around the hook.

5. In similar fashion, tie a second bunch of bucktail, a little shorter, over the first, leaving a little distance between the first and second ties.

6. Add a second thin spread of flash over the hair.

7. Now tie in a slightly shorter bunch of hair in a contrasting color (or the same, if you prefer a solid-color fly). Note that this hair should be a little shorter still and tied in a little closer to the second than the second was to the first.

The additional bunches of bucktail should be tied successively closer as you work up the shank.

8. Cut another bunch of the red bucktail. This photo shows the sections of the bucktail from which the hair is taken. As with the white, the first ties come from lower down on the tail, the later, shorter ones more from the tip. This will give the best taper and form to the fly, while utilizing the hair most effectively; you won't waste the long fibers on the shorter ties at the front of the fly.

9. The second bunch of red bucktail tied in.

10. The third bunch tied in, moving gradually up the shank.

11. Add a fourth bunch. Note that the fourth bunch is made of shorter fibers yet and is tied in a bit closer to the third red tie than the third was to the second.

12. Tie in the fifth and last bunch of hair just behind the hook eye. For this fly, we used two bunches of white and five red, although this may vary according to the length of the hook you use and the amount of hair you tie in.

13. Add prism eyes, whip off the thread, and coat the wraps. Here we used eyes with small tabs, which can be securely attached with the thread. If you use regular round eyes, you can secure them to the bucktail with a drop of cyanoacrylate, like Zap-A-Gap or Krazy Glue. (Actual size, 8 1/4 inches)

THE INNER FLASH TECHNIQUE

Inner Flash is not the designation of a particular fly, but rather a tying technique that can be applied to many Pop Fleyes or other patterns to improve them. In effect, the 3D employs the idea of Inner Flash. It is really as simple as tying the flash material under the hair or fibers of the body or wing. Many patterns call for flash to be tied on the back or side of the fly, on top of the wing hair or fiber, and usually together in a small bunch. This method concentrates the flash in one area, and often the wet tinsel clings to itself and tangles when casting. By tying tinsel or other flash with the Inner Flash method, you can give your flies a more subtle flash, even an eerie glow, and completely eliminate tangling.

See page 103 for additional variations of the generic pattern.

Inner Flash (Generic Baitfish Pattern)

Materials

Standard-length stainless hook
Fine monofilament thread
Kinky Fiber or other synthetic hair
Comes Alive or other flash
Polar Fiber or other bright synthetic
3D eyes

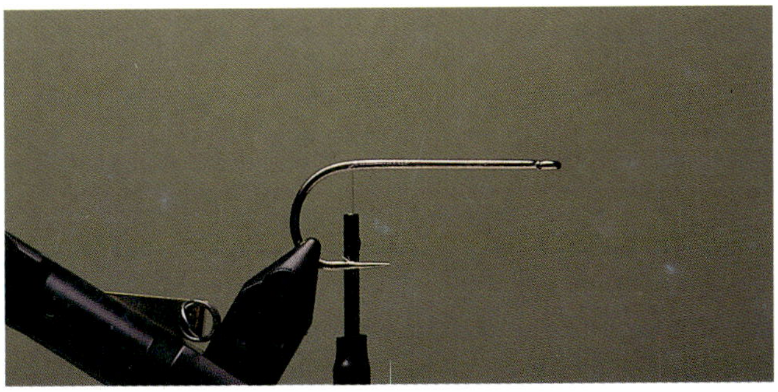

1. Attach the thread to the hook near the bend.

2. Attach limp flash, approximately one and a half to two times the length of the shank, cinching it in the middle as shown, and spreading it around the shank. In this sample, we are using Comes Alive.

3. Fold the front ends of the flash back and fasten securely with the thread.

4. Add some synthetic hair, Kinky Fiber in this case, about the length of the flash, also distributed around the shank.

5. Add a second, sparse layer of flash around the fly, over the fiber. Make these strands shorter than the first.

6. Fold back the front ends and tie them down as before.

7. Add a third, shorter, and still more sparse complement of flash in similar fashion.

8. Tie a small bunch of orange or red Polar Fiber or other material to simulate the gills or add a splash of color, if desired.

9. Trim the front tips of the long fibers, fold back the short ends, and tie them down.

10. Attach a final, sparse collar of the Kinky Fiber or other material.

11. After building up the head, add 3D eyes and coat the head with epoxy. (Fly shown actual size.)

Inner Flash (Brown Baby Bunker)

(Actual size, 3 1/8 inches)

Inner Flash (Green)

(Actual size, 4 1/8 inches)

Cotton Candy

We tied this fly originally with Big Fly Fiber, also known as Hairabou, and still often tie it this way. Bozo Hair, shown in the sample here, is used as an alternative. It is a bit stiffer and has more body to retain a fuller form and silhouette. Other hairs can also be used to make this large but simple fly. Invariably, old, traditional patterns tied for such large imitations tended to be bulky, retained too much water, and were difficult to cast. The Cotton Candy fly gives the illusion of bulk while producing a relatively sparse fly that is eminently castable. You can make a very large Cotton Candy, up to 18 inches, using the two-vise method described later in this chapter. Since this is a large fly, any hair or fiber that retains much water will make for difficult casting. Try to use fibers that shed water, like the two mentioned. With these hairs, most of the water is shed on the first backcast, so that although there is some wind resistance on the forward cast, the weight is not a problem, and almost any Cotton Candy, other than the very largest, which are used for billfish, can be cast comfortably on a 10- or 11-weight rod.

Materials

Trey Combs or other large-gap saltwater hook
Fine monofilament thread
Bozo Hair or Big Fly Fiber
Pearl Flashabou or other lightweight flash
Self-sticking prism eyes, large
Sheep fleece

Because of the design, even a foot-long Cotton Candy is not difficult to fish on an 11-weight rod.

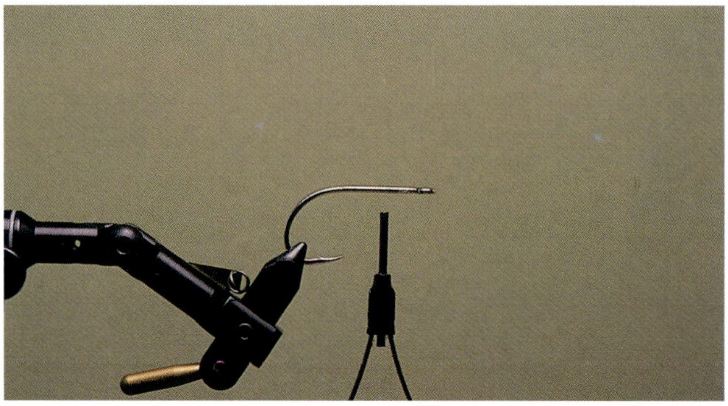

1. Start with the thread attached back a bit from the eye. Here we use a 6/0 Trey Combs hook.

2. Tie Bozo Hair at midshank, spread around the shank, not just on top. Comb out the hair with a comb to eliminate any tangles in the material.

3. Put a little pearl Flashabou over the hair.

4. Add some light blue Bozo Hair, the length of the body, only on top of the fly.

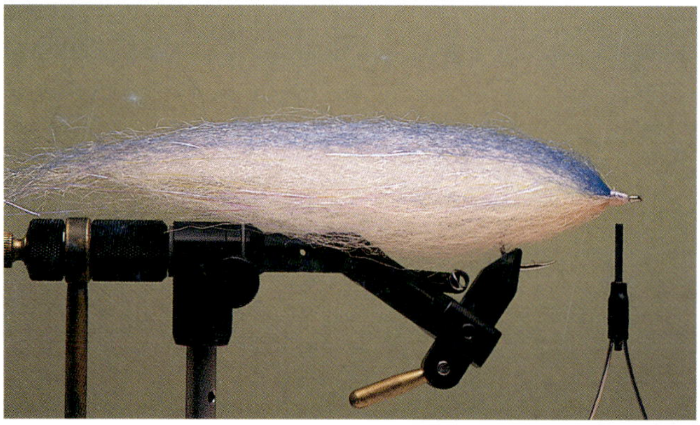

5. Tie some pale pink Bozo Hair on the bottom, a little shorter than the blue.

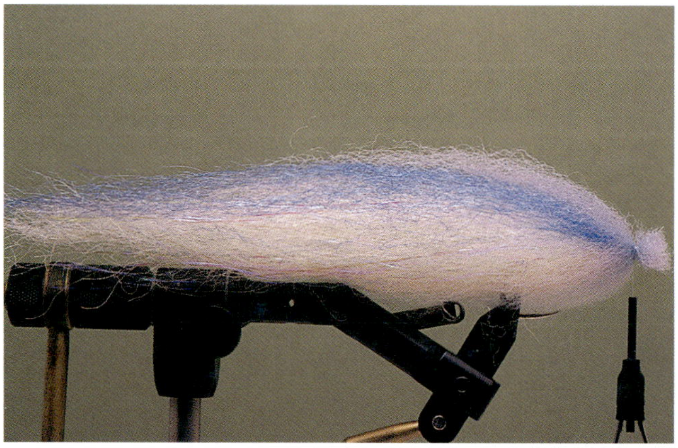

6. Add a fine veil of pale blue sheep fleece over the front of the fly to fill out and round the front, as well as give subtle color without adding weight.

7. Trim the excess fleece, and take some extra thread turns.

8. Tie off the thread, and add large eyes, using a spot of glue on the back. (Actual size, 7 7/8 inches)

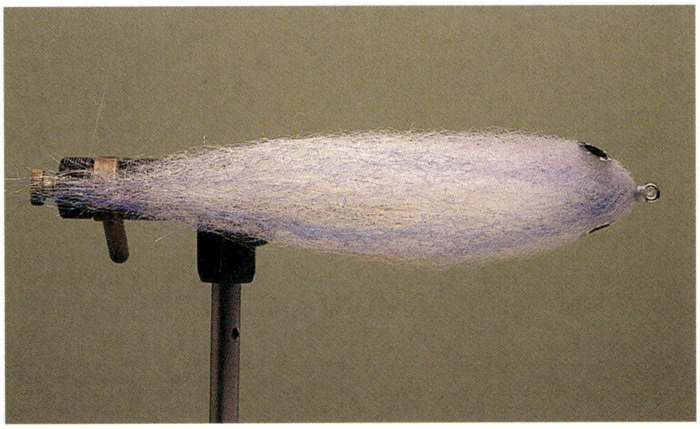

9. Top view of the finished Cotton Candy, showing full form and taper.

By blending different shades of hair and fleece, you can produce more lifelike color combinations. Note the subtle coloration of the Cotton Candies on pages 7 and 103.

Semper Fleye

An earlier version of this was called the Jersey Knight. The Semper Fleye uses some of the most traditional materials—namely, two kinds of saddle hackle and a bit of bucktail. No synthetic fibers, epoxy, or silicone are used, not even tinsel or eyes. Creating this great striped bass fly depends on simply manipulating the materials effectively. The Semper Fleye relies on the mass of collar hackles to give it bulk and buoyancy, but most importantly, it uses a novel method of attaching the long tail hackles to give improved action. Tying hackles "in the round" or "clock wound" also makes for better action in many other flies, such as Lefty's Deceiver.

The two types of saddle hackles used in the Semper Fleye.

Materials
Standard-length saltwater hook
Fine monofilament thread
Bucktail
Long, slender saddle hackles
Wide, webby saddle hackles

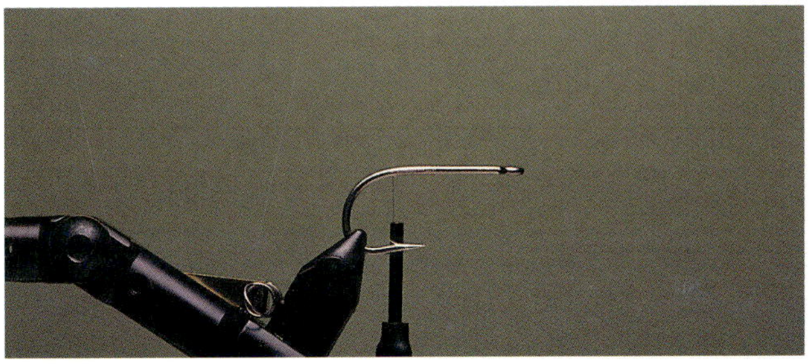

1. Begin with the thread attached at the bend of the hook.

2. Tie in a bunch of bucktail, about one and a half times the length of the hook shank, distributing the fibers around the shank.

3. Tie one of the long, fairly limp saddle hackles on the far side of the fly, dull side facing inward. Leave some of the fluffy webbing at the base of the stem.

4. Tie a second hackle on the near side.

5. Add a third hackle, flat on the top.

The hackles, tied in one at a time, should be spaced evenly around the shank.

6. Continue adding hackles, one at a time, in between the first ones. In all, you will probably use six to eight hackles, depending on fly size. Hackles arranged in this fashion produce much better action than hackles tied flat to the sides of the fly. Each waves or breathes individually, instead of being impeded by the others.

7. Just ahead of the wing hackles, attach a long, webby saddle hackle, dull side to the rear.

8. Wind the hackle forward several turns.

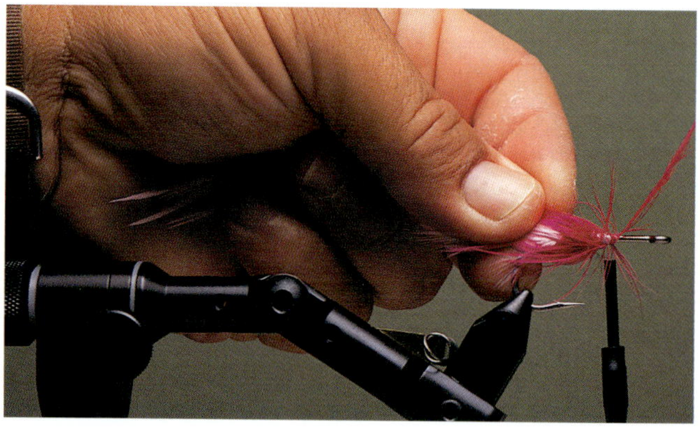

9. Tie off the hackle.

10. Wrap the thread to the back slightly, over the base of the fibers, in order to pack the fibers and push them rearward.

11. Repeat the procedure with additional hackles until the hackle collar fills the shank. Tie off and coat the head with head cement. (Fly shown actual size.)

The black Semper Fleye is an excellent night fly for stripers. (Actual size, 7 inches)

Here's the ideal time and place to fish the black Semper Fleye.

BOB'S BANGERS

All anglers, whether fishing flies or plugs, thrill to topwater action, and popping bugs, or poppers, have been used since the earliest days of the sport. Bob's Banger is another example of form following function. For years we used the Ka-Boom-Boom, which was born on our home waters of Barnegat Bay. It's still a sentimental favorite with us, but the Banger has many advantages over cork, balsa, and even many foam-bodied poppers. Its beauty lies in the simplicity of its design. The Banger requires no paint, no glue, no shaping or sanding, yet it has flash, color, durability, pops better, and tracks straighter (without "crabbing") than any other popper we have used. It also allows a different action. Importantly, it is tier-friendly. In an evening, even moderately talented fly tiers can produce a season's supply.

Of the many foam materials available, we find that Live Body, by Dale Clemens Custom Tackle, has the best texture, density, and buoyancy. The marriage of the foam body and the Witchcraft reflective tape is the key to the Banger's durability. Both materials are quite tough, but teeth of bluefish and other species will readily cut unprotected foam. On the other hand, the tape, when used over a hard surface, will also show scars, scrapes, and cuts. Here, however, the tape wrapped around the body protects the foam, while the foam simultaneously protects the tape by yielding to the fish's jaw pressure. The bug, instead of being bitten in half, which often happens with cork or wood types, usually only is indented by the bites. In time, the indentations slowly diminish as the foam resumes its normal shape. While developing this bug years ago, we caught six large bluefish on one. We left the bug with Capt. Mike Hintlian of Massachusetts, who then caught several more and mailed the bug to us. Repeating this routine several times affirmed for us the efficacy of the lure's design.

Bob's Banger

Materials

Long-shank saltwater hook, preferably 6X
Fine monofilament thread
Heavy rod wrapping thread, D or E
Bucktail
Cactus Chenille or Estaz
Live Body foam cylinders 3/8 inch and up
Large, self-sticking prism eyes

1. It is important to use thick nylon rod wrapping thread. Color is immaterial.

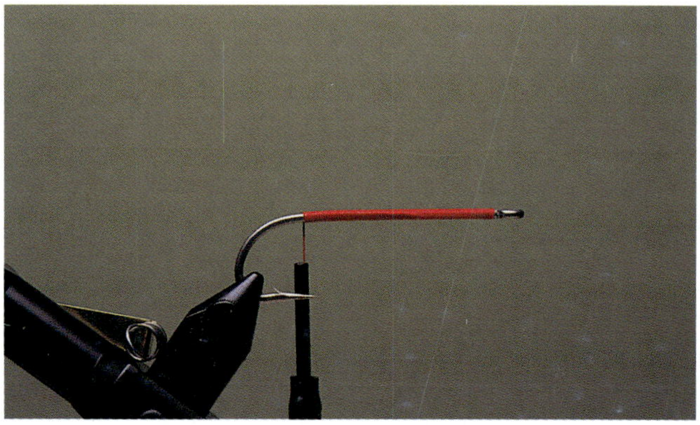

2. Layer the shank of a long hook with the thread.

3. Attach a bunch of bucktail, about the length of the hook shank, near the bend. Don't extend the butts of the hair farther forward than shown.

4. Tie in a length of Estaz or Cactus Chenille.

5. Wrap the chenille forward tightly and tie it off.

6. Coat the thread with head cement and let dry. This will protect the thread wraps from wear and make it easier to slide on the popper head.

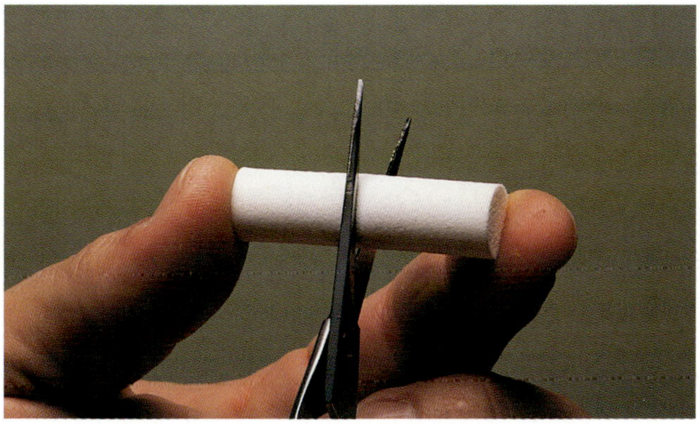

7. Cut a cylinder of Live Body in half (about 1 inch long).

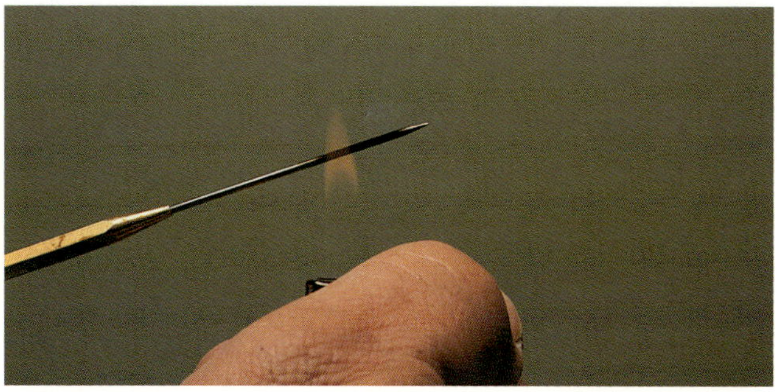

8. Heat the point of your bodkin with a lighter or match.

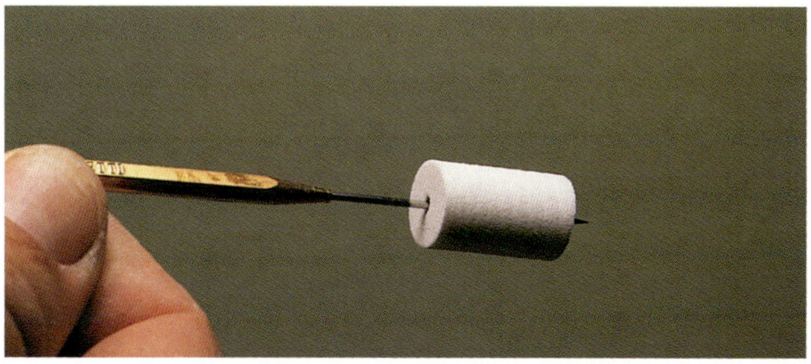

9. Sear a hole dead center through the foam head with the hot needle. Don't enlarge the hole. The foam head should fit snugly onto the shank.

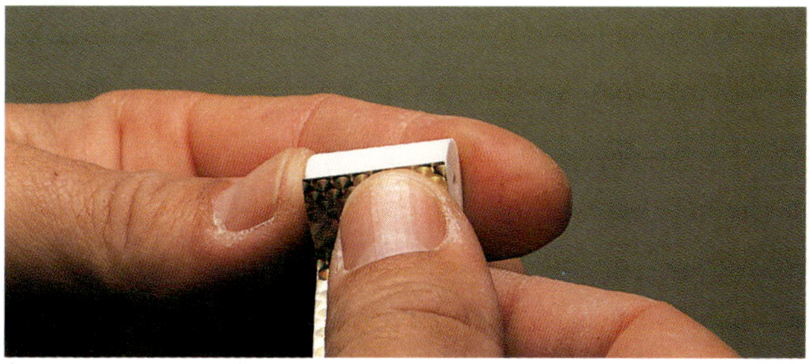

10. Wrap a piece of metallic tape around the head.

11. Make certain the tape overlaps itself, about one and a half wraps around the head.

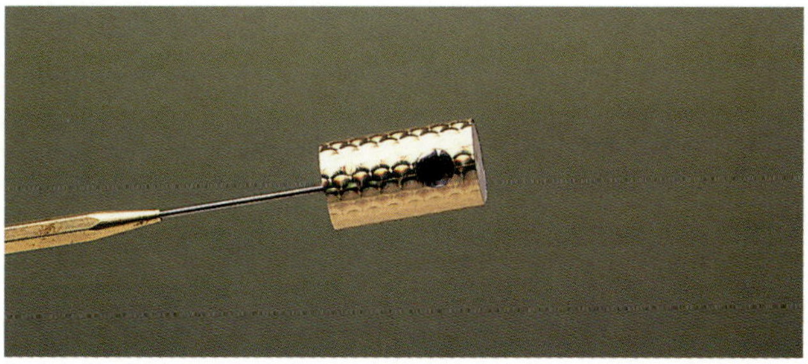

12. The finished head with eyes added. Crease the eyes sharply in the center before applying them so that they hug the contour of the head.

13. Slide the head onto the hook shank. (Fly shown actual size.)

14. You can easily interchange head sizes and colors.

Note: If the hole enlarges with wear and the head fits loosely, you can always fasten it in place with a spot of glue, although you will sacrifice the interchangeability feature. Another option would be to sear a second hole near the edge of the cylinder and glue the hook in place so that it is in a more conventional position, near the bottom of the head, but this will change the Banger's action.

Fishing Tip: Fishing Bob's Banger

To get the most out of Bob's Banger, or any popping bug for that matter, learn to work the lure with your line hand, not your rod. Point the rod toward the popper, get any slack out of the rod, and give a sharp tug with your line hand. It's all right to complement this with a quick, short flick of the rod tip, but don't count on the rod tip to impart most of the action to the lure. Sometimes subtle pops work better than loud, noisy ones. Another effective retrieve involves giving the line a long, sweeping pull as soon as the Banger touches the water at the end of your cast. The fly will dig in with a loud plunging noise and swim under the surface, leaving a long stream of bubbles in its wake. When it bobs back to the surface, wait a second and then repeat. Finally, the design of the Banger makes it easy to fish as a slider. Simply pull the line more gently and steadily, without popping. Some poppers, which have hooks placed at the bottom of the body and deeply cupped faces, will "crab" side to side when pulled hard, making a straight line movement difficult. When fishing in a blitz, particularly of bluefish, cast into the carnage and simply let the fly float with no movement or action at all. You will be surprised at the strikes you will draw if you are simply patient. Bluefish chop many baitfish in half and like to clean up dead and wounded fish or portions of them. This is also a highly effective strategy when fishing for false albacore behind shrimp boats. The commercial fishermen discard all sorts of baitfish and mollusks, and the fish lie in the wake of the stern gobbling up whatever is tossed overboard. Cast a Banger into the wash and let it bob around but don't work it—and hang on.

This striper crashed a Bob's Banger at sunset at Lobsterville Beach, Martha's Vineyard.

Offshore Banger

The Offshore Banger has no hook attached, rather like a tube fly. It is simply a larger Banger that can be used inshore too for species like jacks and trevally, which like a lot of noise. To use it, insert heavy mono through the center hole and attach the hook of your choice. Below are the steps for making a large Offshore Banger head.

1. Using an entire 2-inch-long, large Live Body cylinder, mark the center point and about eight points around the perimeter with a marking pen.

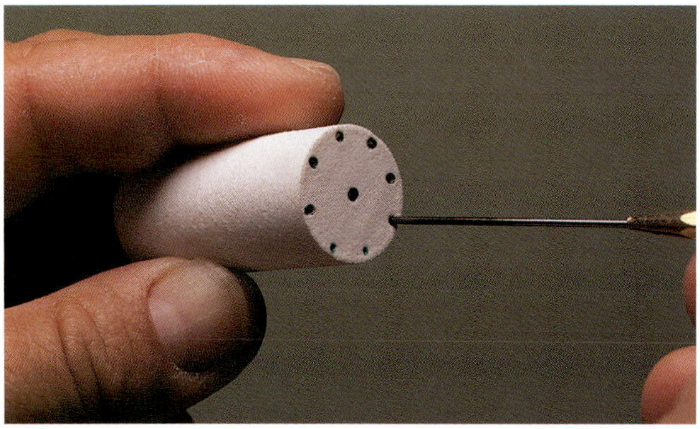

2. Sear the center hole as above, and simply poke holes into the perimeter about an inch deep.

3. Cut the base from a large saddle hackle, leaving some of the fluffy marabou at the base.

4. Moisten the fibers and stroke them into line.

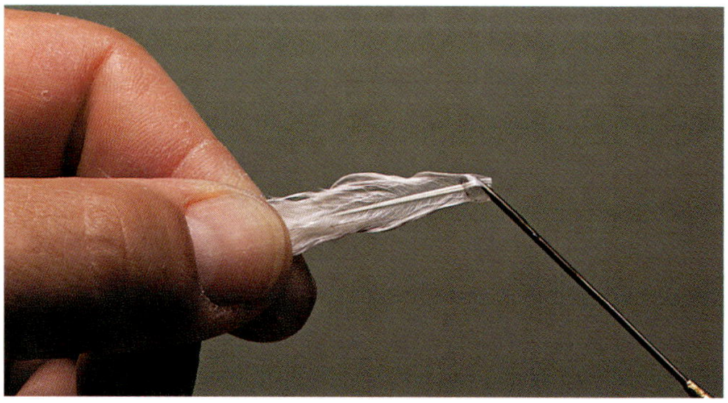

5. Coat about an inch of the hackle stem with five-minute epoxy.

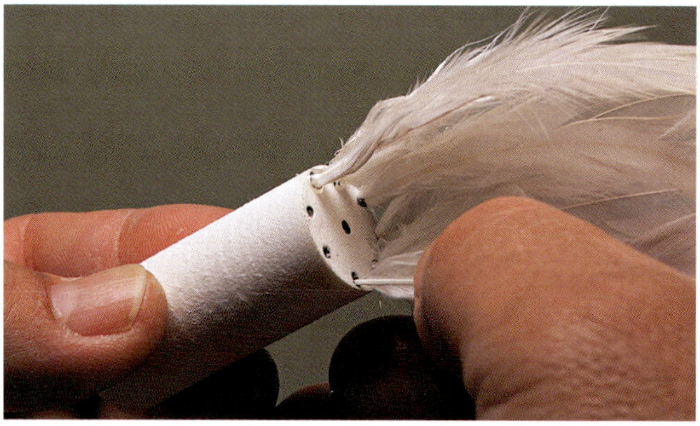

6. Insert the hackle stem, dull side inward, into one of the perimeter holes. Move to the next hole and repeat the operation.

7. The Offshore Banger head with all eight hackles in place.

8. Add metallic tape and large eyes, as described in steps 10-12 of Bob's Banger, and the head is finished. Insert heavy mono through the center hole and attach the hook of your choice. (Fly shown actual size.)

Small Banger Tube Fly

This smaller version is similar to the large head just described. Wrap a skirt of metallic tape around the Live Body and, with your scissors, cut lengthwise slits into the material. Add the regular strip of tape and eyes to the head.

TYING WITH TWO VISES

We conclude our book with the same technique described at the opening. This technique addresses several tying problems. Bob first experimented with it thirty years ago. Rather than tying all the materials directly onto the hook, some are attached to a section of monofilament, which in turn is fastened to the hook, to which additional materials are then added. Using this method, we have constructed flies measuring a full eighteen inches, which were comfortable to cast on an 11-weight rod. Granted, such enormous creations are seldom employed, but when they are needed, here is an effective way to make then. In addition, the technique can be used to make more modest-size, flexible flies with great action.

First, stretch a piece of moderately stiff monofilament, 20- or 30-pound-test, tightly between two vises. Monofilament "straights" work best. These are precut, straight sections typically sold in tackle shops, especially in coastal areas. They are usually about 2 1/2 or 3 feet in length and used by surf fishermen for making bait rigs. These work better than softer, coiled monofilament, which must be cut to length and straightened. Coiled mono is also usually softer than we like for fly extensions. Set up two vises, with the jaws facing in the same direction, as shown in the photo, but about 2 feet or more apart. Clamp one end of the mono into one of the vises, pull it tight, and clamp the mono into the other vise. If it vibrates like a banjo string when plucked, you've got it right.

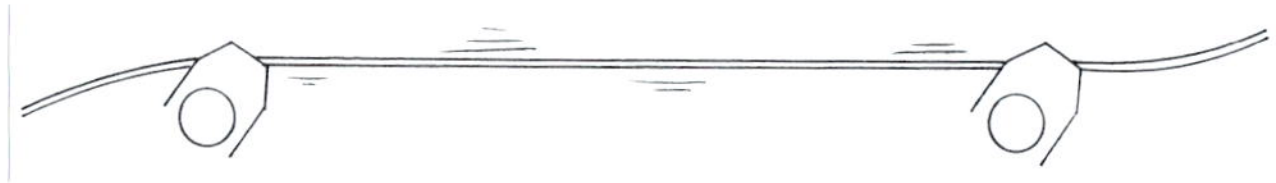

The mono should be stretched taut between the vises, like a banjo string.

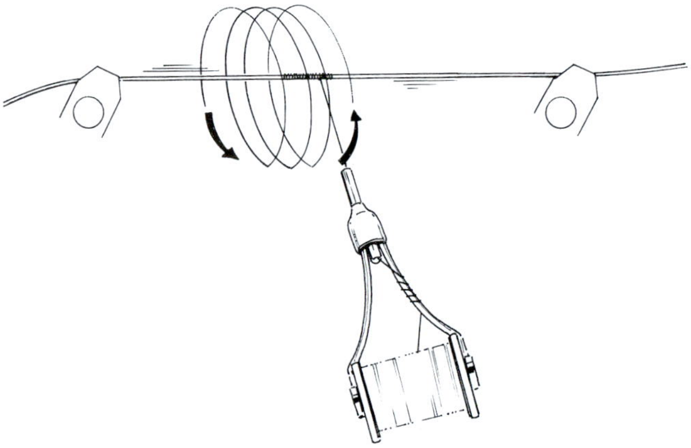

Flip the bobbin smartly so that the momentum causes it to wind tightly around the mono in a series of wraps. Repeat if you need more wraps.

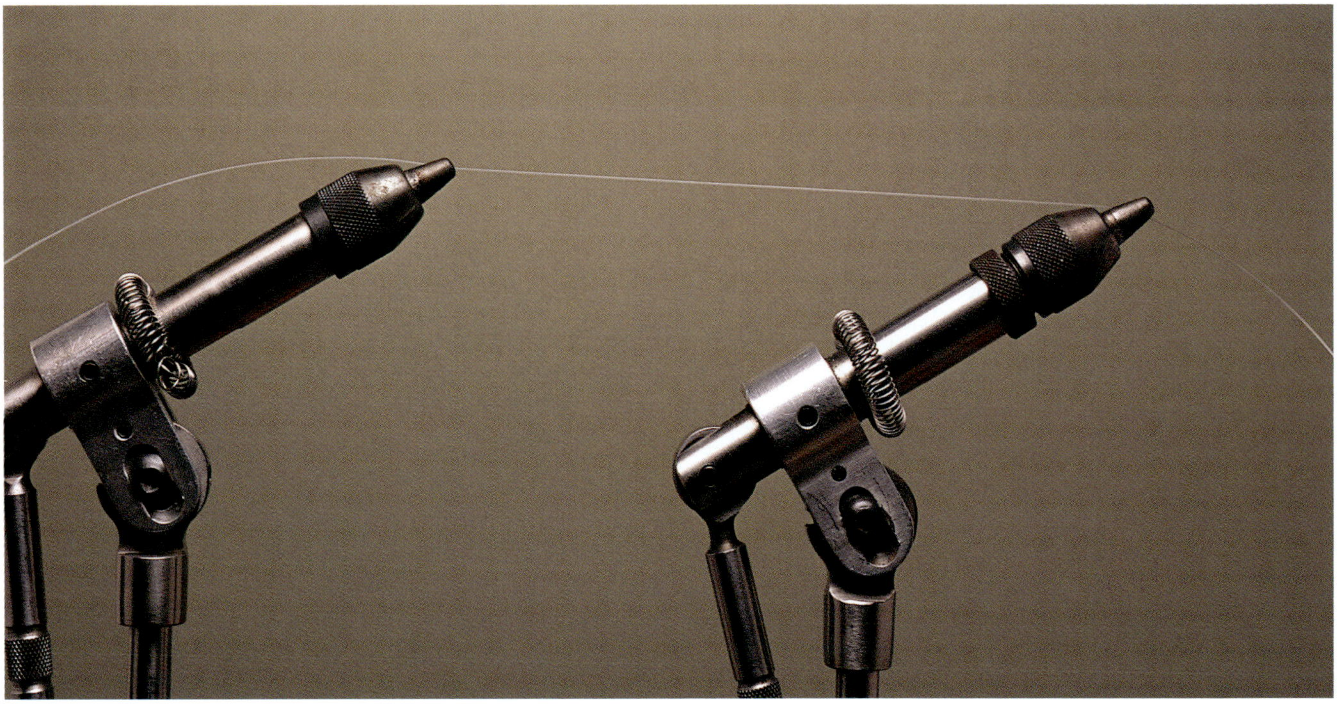

Stretch stiff monofilament between two vises with the jaws facing the same direction, as above, but at least two feet apart.

Obviously, you can't wrap your bobbin around the material as you normally would by rotating your hand around the vise. Hold one end of the tying thread with your materials hand, and loosely flip the bobbin around the mono a few times to anchor the thread. It is most important that you wrap the thread around one leg of your bobbin about four times as shown in the photos so that when you flip the bobbin, no thread feeds from the spool. To attach material, hold the material against the mono as if it were the hook shank, and briskly flip the bobbin so that it swings around the strand of mono, tightly fastening the material to it. After the bobbin makes about five or six wraps, you can feed more thread by hand from the bobbin, and repeat the process.

When tying between vises, you cannot tie off the thread using a normal whip-finish operation, whether by hand or with one of the many tools on the market. Here is the method we use.

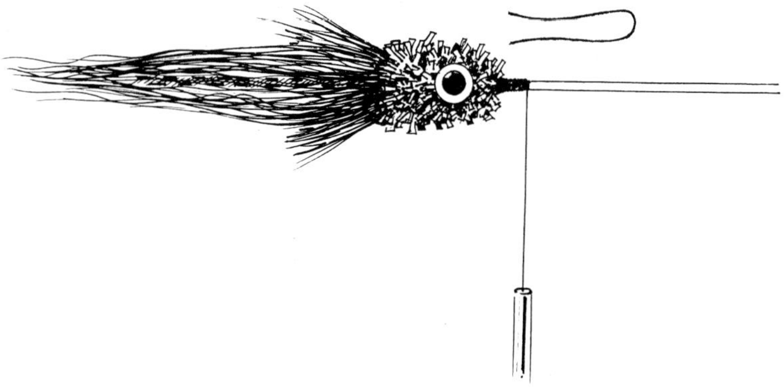

When you've finished tying the squid head, take a few inches of heavier thread, double it, and lay it on the heavy mono.

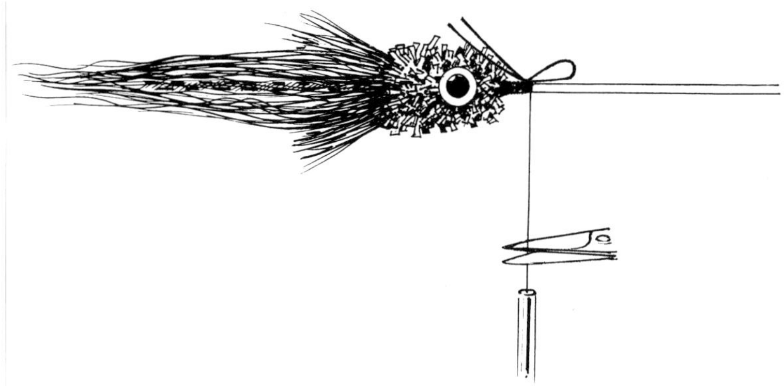

Fasten it with five or six final wraps and snip the tying thread. Hold onto the loose end so it doesn't unravel.

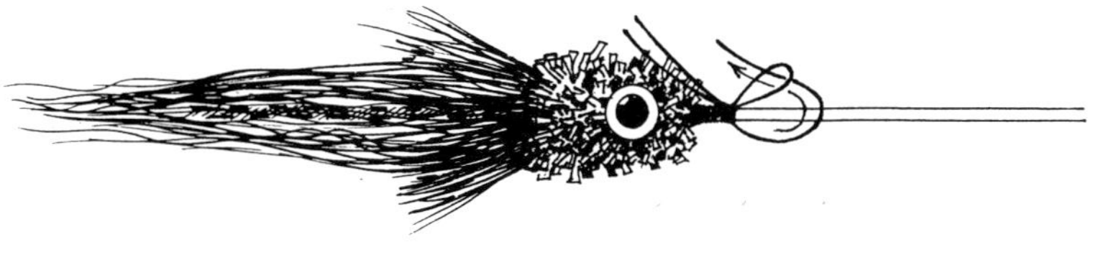

Pass the loose end through the heavy loop.

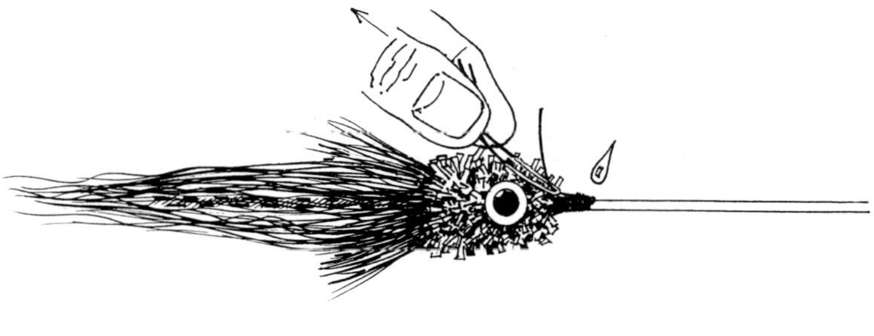

Pull the heavy loop out, which will pull the tying thread underneath the final wraps. This is precisely the technique you would use to attach a guide to a rod.

Shady Lady Squid

An early version of the Shady Lady Squid was pictured and described in Frank Wentink's *Salt Water Fly Tying* (Lyons and Burford, 1991). Here we show a greatly improved version, made with the two-vise tying method to tie the head and tentacles on the monofilament. It's a good idea to tie several heads in succession along the monofilament and cut them apart as you need them. Leave about 3 or 4 inches of mono protruding from the back of the head for attachment to the hook.

Materials

Tiemco 911S or other long-shank saltwater hook
Fine monofilament thread
Stiff monofilament, 20 to 30 pound-test
Cactus Chenille or Estaz
Slender saddle hackles
Self-sticking prism eyes
Sheep fleece or ram's wool

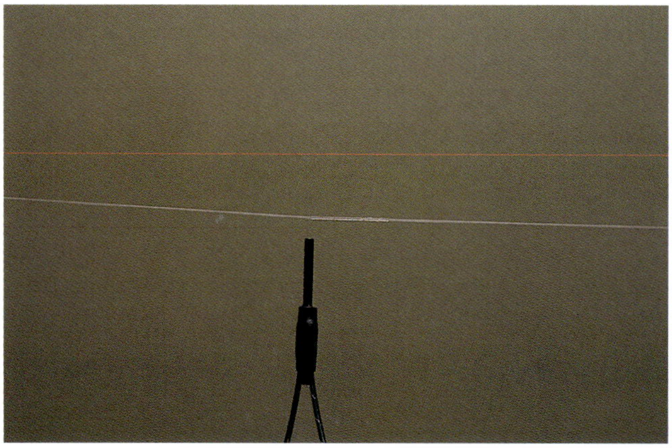

1. Base wrap a layer of thread along an inch of the heavy mono, which is stretched between the two vises, as described on page 114.

2. Attach a piece of Estaz or Cactus Chenille

3. Wrap the Estaz around the mono for about 1/2 inch, tie down, and trim off.

4. Mark eight or ten saddle hackles with a permanent black felt marking pen. Leave some of the marabou fluff at the base of the hackles.

5. Attach the hackles one or two at a time. Here we show the first two tied to the mono.

6. Continue adding hackles "around the clock," as described for the Semper Fleye, until all hackles are attached to the mono. Trim and tie down the stems.

7. Attach a piece of Estaz.

8. Wrap the Estaz along the mono for an inch or two and tie off. Add eyes, secured with a drop of Zap-A-Gap or Krazy Glue.

9. Two finished Shady Lady Squid heads tied on monofilament between two vises. We generally create a "daisy chain" of up to six heads in advance.

10. To complete a Shady Lady Squid, cut the monofilament close to the "mouth" of the squid in the center of the hackles, leaving about 4 inches or more extending from the back of the head. Attach the mono to the hook shank.

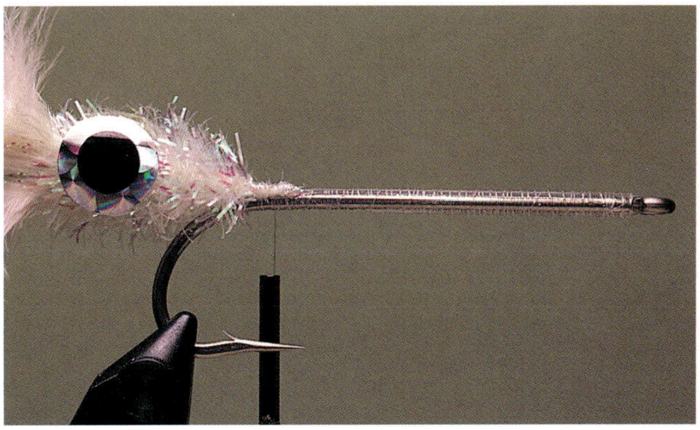

11. For added security, especially if you want to add a stinger hook, you can pass the mono through the hook eye and wrap it securely with thread, as shown.

12. Attach another piece of Estaz or Cactus Chenille.

13. Wrap the chenille along the mono and continue around the hook shank to the eye. Tie it down and trim the excess.

14. Just behind the hook eye, tie a veil of sheep fleece, like a shroud, around the body. It should extend to the squid eye.

15. Trim, tie off, and coat the head. Here's a finished Shady Lady Squid after the fleece has been trimmed and the thread tied off and coated. (Actual size, 8 1/2 inches)

Additional squid patterns are also described in the chapters on epoxy and silicone, as well as under 3D flies in this chapter.

Fishing Tip: Fishing the Shady Lady Squid

From studying underwater films of the swimming motion of many baits, we have decided that, in most cases, squid flies should be retrieved in fairly long, moderately fast pulls. In between strips, the fly will settle or sink only slightly, and in a generally level attitude, enhanced by the fluttering of the feather tentacles.

When fishing a squid fly, try to simulate the stop-and-go darting action of the natural.

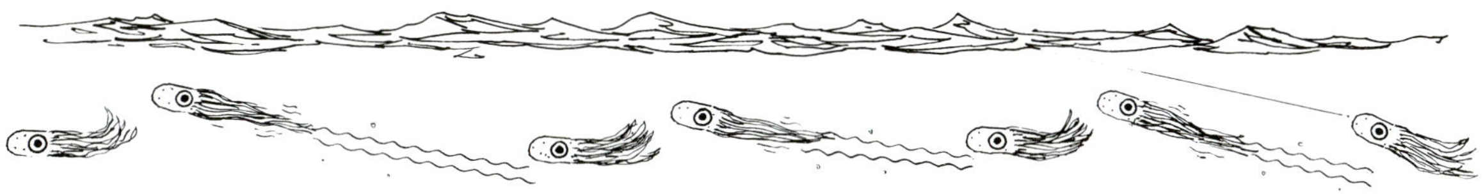

A modified Shady Lady Squid took this 39-inch bass at night.

Offshore Cotton Candy

Earlier, we described a Cotton Candy tied with Bozo Hair. When fishing for sailfish and marlin, some anglers want truly large flies, yet with castability. Using the two-vise technique described on page 114, we create such lures by first attaching a full bunch of Big Fish Fiber to a strand of fairly stiff mono or fluorocarbon; 100-pound is not too heavy. Since this fly is so large, it would take an inordinate number of wraps around the mono to secure the hair neatly. When making large flies for billfish, we have no qualms about leaving the tie-down area apparently rough and unfinished, provided that it is secure.

Materials

Trey Combs or other large-gap saltwater hook
Fine monofilament thread
Big Fly Fiber
Large, self-sticking prism eyes
Stiff monofilament, 80 to 100 pound-test

1. Dress the Big Fly Fiber around the mono stretched between vises, as described on page 114.

2. Cut the mono and then attach it securely to the hook, usually 6/0 or larger.

3. Dress another bunch of fiber around the hook shank. The completed fly can be upward of 18 inches.

As an option, you can tie a stinger hook to the mono in the rear bunch of hair. Many anglers feel this is a decided advantage when fishing for billfish, large dorado, and other saltwater fish.

You can adapt the two-vise technique to add a stinger hook to a huge offshore Cotton Candy.

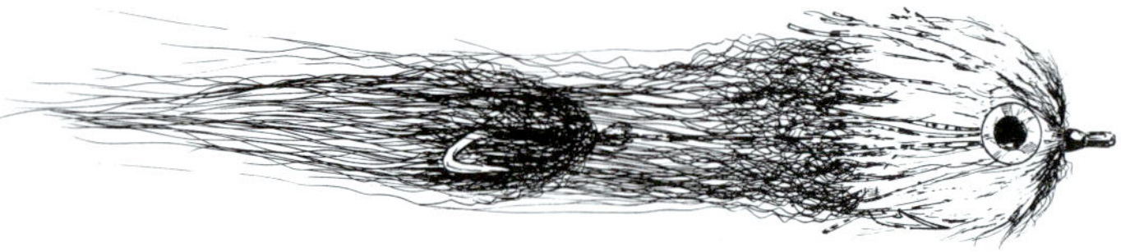

Practical offshore flies up to 18 inches, tied using the two-vise method.

Fishing Tip: Casting Large Flies

Fly lines with longer front tapers and longer bellies work fine for Surf Candies and similar smaller flies. However, when casting bulky flies and air-resistant creations like popping bugs and the Cotton Candy, use lines with shorter front tapers and heavier bellies, usually designated as saltwater tapers. Also, a 9- or 10-weight line may not have enough mass and momentum to transport a large fly. Some anglers are intimidated by 11- and 12-weight outfits, but a heavier rod and line combination will often make presentation and casting a lot easier, rather than more difficult. Sometimes just overlining your rod will help—using a size or two heavier line than that recommended for your rod. Also, tie these flies with synthetic materials that don't readily absorb water. Nonabsorbent material and high line speed on your backcast will shed most of the water to the rear, and your forward delivery will be much easier.

Most important, casting large, bulky, wind-resistant, or heavy flies calls for an adjustment in your casting stroke. A longer arm and rod motion will make *any* cast easier, so when you need help, don't restrict your cast to the brief, staccato motions you would use when flicking a dry fly on a trout stream. Take your rod back more to the side, rather than directly overhead, and make a long stroke, using a full-arm extension to the rear if necessary. This gives more time to generate your hand acceleration, which loads the rod.

Use a longer rod and arm extension to cast large flies, even to the point of turning and extending your arm full length to the rear.

Index of Patterns